D0888080

CASE STUDIES IN
CULTURAL ANTHROPOLOGY

GENERAL EDITORS

George and Louise Spindler

STANFORD UNIVERSITY

LIFELINES

WITHDRAWN

LIFELINES

Black Families in Chicago

By

JOYCE ASCHENBRENNER

Southern Illinois University

HOLT, RINEHART AND WINSTON, INC.

NEW YORK CHICAGO SAN FRANCISCO ATLANTA
DALLAS MONTREAL TORONTO LONDON SYDNEY

Cover: Golden Wedding Anniversary

Copyright © 1975 by Holt, Rinehart and Winston, Inc.
All rights reserved
Library of Congress Catalog Card Number: 74–19871
ISBN: 0–03–012826–9
Printed in the United States of America
5 6 7 8 9   059   9 8 7 6 5 4 3 2 1

Foreword

About the Series

These case studies in cultural anthropology are designed to bring to students in the social sciences insights into the richness and complexity of human life as it is lived in different ways and in different places. They are written by men and women who have lived in the societies they write about, and who are professionally trained as observers and interpreters of human behavior. The authors are also teachers, and in writing their books they have kept the students who will read them foremost in their minds. It is our belief that when an understanding of ways of life very different from one's own is gained, abstractions and generalizations about social structure, cultural values, subsistence techniques, and other universal categories of human social behavior become meaningful.

About the Author

Joyce Aschenbrenner received her Ph.D. from the University of Minnesota in 1967, after having completed an M.A. in Philosophy at Tulane University. She has worked among Minnesota Chippewa, in Muslim communities of India and Pakistan, and in Black communities in Chicago and Southern Illinois. She is "action-oriented" in her approach, and has participated in Black and Native American community centers as a volunteer worker. She seeks new social perspectives by means of dialogue between social participants. She is presently teaching and conducting research at Southern Illinois University at Edwardsville and belongs to the Edwardsville chapter of the NAACP, the local Black organization in which White supporters play an active role.

About the Book

Many analysts of the Black family in the United States interpret it as primarily a product of slavery, poverty, and prejudice; as an adaptation to conditions that have left it stripped of resources for the proper socialization of the young or the satisfaction of adult members. The emphasis tends to be upon its matrifocal characteristics and on shifting conjugal alliances. Joyce Aschenbrenner takes a different view. She stresses the extended kin group rather than the nuclear family that is the norm among middle-class Whites. She shows how the consanguineal relationships are emphasized, as much as, or more than the nuclear ones in social and economic interaction, and how the mother-daughter tie is of particular signifi-

30081

cance. Paradoxically from the White point of view the deemphasis on the conjugal tie does not mean a deemphasis on the male-female love relationship. The
description in Chapter 2 of the love relationship will leave some readers envious
—not because these relationships are trouble-free, but because they are intense and
satisfying. The need of women for men and of men for women is acknowledged
and extends beyond sex, although the sexual dimension continues to be important.

The picture of the Black family that Dr. Aschenbrenner gives us is quite different from one that shows it as barren and devoid of satisfactions. What we are
shown instead is a rich, complex, and functional family pattern, which is an
integral part of Black culture, and is created out of many diverse elements from
the past as well as from the present.

The strategy used by the author to present this picture is to provide detailed
information on the social drama in Black family life in the context of Black
culture in one northern urban center. As she says, ". . . this treatment is not
written so that one can skip over details and concentrate on generalizations;
rather, the technique is to build up a mosaic of social reality through the juxtaposition of life experiences, in an attempt to convey a complexity that cannot be
grasped through the bald statement of fact or theory."

The strategy, as the reader will discover, is quite effective.

GEORGE AND LOUISE SPINDLER
General Editors

Stanford, California

Preface

This account of Black family life is the product of a series of events, which were initiated when a Black fellow graduate student "got on my case." Through this rather traumatic, but very enlightening experience, I was ultimately led to forego my planned specialization in Muslims in the subcontinent. I turned instead to an intriguing and distinctive aspect of my own society, developed by its Black members. I found myself playing primarily a role of observer and, whenever possible, of helper in the coalition between Blacks and liberals in the late 1960s; the rewards of this experience and of my subsequent research, in terms of insight and knowledge of the realities of American society, have been great.

The present study is based on observation and interviews, over a period of one year, of ten individuals and their extended families, as well as on informal discussions and participation in events with friends and acquaintances. In important instances, I came to know informants through social networks, stemming from my work in a Black community center. The directors of The Way—Gwen Jones-Davis and Sylvester Davis—gave me the impetus to overcome my ignorance of an important aspect of American culture. Raymond T. Smith and David M. Schneider, directors of the project in which I took part, afforded me tools of analysis as well as sustenance. Finally, Ethel Lawrence, Henrietta Williams, and William Holmes have given me invaluable assistance and friendship, and the Black people of Chicago have given me a "special feeling" toward their "Black Metropolis."

JOYCE ASCHENBRENNER

Edwardsville, Ill.
September 1974

ix

Contents

Introduction

For decades social scientists have been writing about the instability of the Black family. To explain its infirmity, apologists have referred to the breakup of families during the time of slavery and to the poverty of the Northern ghetto.[1] Most writers, whether sympathetic or critical, have assumed that the Black family is disorganized; they have differed only on what they view as the cause for this disorganization.

As a student I had accepted the stereotype of the Black family; I became aware of its misrepresentation later, when a radical change in my environment occurred (in anthropological terms, the "rite of passage"). In my initial fieldwork in Pakistan, where I studied village social and political organization, I encountered an outside view of the American family that ultimately led me to reevaluate my own assumptions about the Black family. From the point of view of Pakistanis, the family in the United States is weak or even nonexistent. Pakistani women were critical of American women for working and neglecting their children. The practice of hiring a stranger to babysit was abhorrent to them: Where were the grandparents or aunts and uncles? Imagine a widow or a divorcee bringing up children by herself. What was the matter with her husband's brothers? Wouldn't her own family help her out? The high divorce rate in this country was repeatedly mentioned, as well as the lack of respect for parents and older people. The practice of staying in a hotel when traveling or visiting was also unthinkable; there were always relatives or friends who would be happy to share what they had, and insulted if you did not accept.

Obviously, the Pakistanis were looking at families from a different viewpoint than were the social scientists; otherwise, the Black family would not have been singled out so consistently in the literature as an example of family breakdown. On the contrary, as I worked among Black families in Chicago from 1969 to 1970, I found that the quality of relationships and the extent of obligations between family members were more similar to families in Pakistan than to most families I had known in the United States. My previous experience, while working at a Black community center in Minneapolis, had prepared me for a different outlook and value orientation among Blacks; however, I had not observed Black families for a great length

[1] Cf. Lee Rainwater and William L. Yancy, eds., *The Moynihan Report and the Politics of Controversy.* Cambridge, Mass.: M.I.T. Press, 1967; E. Franklin Frazier, *The Negro Family in the United States.* Chicago: University of Chicago Press, 1939.

A fine-looking family

of time and the vitality of Black families as revealed in my interviews was thus unexpected.

I was introduced to the kinship interview techniques developed by David M. Schneider and Raymond T. Smith at the University of Chicago, where I worked as a Research Associate. Schneider had used the same techniques in studying American middle-class families[2]; Smith had investigated the family organization in British Guiana and Jamaica.[3] Together they were expanding their interests to include

[2] See David M. Schneider, *American Kinship: A Cultural Account.* Englewood Cliffs, N.J.: Prentice-Hall, 1968.

[3] Raymond T. Smith, *The Negro Family in British Guiana.* London: Routledge & Kegan Paul, 1956.

lower-class families in Chicago: Blacks, Southern Appalachians, and Puerto Ricans. Since I interviewed Black people in Chicago as a part of this project, I became aware of the large network of relatives surrounding them and the extent of interaction and interdependence among kin.

Discussions of the breakdown of the Black family have usually focused on the marital relationship. This emphasis reflects the overriding importance of the marriage tie in our society, rather than any peculiarity of the Black family. In societies with extended families, other relationships, such as father-son, mother-daughter, or brother-sister, may be more important in terms of social and economic support than that of husband and wife. In Pakistan, a marriage is stable when it is actively supported by the extended kin group in order to maintain the social and economic advantages that were attained through the union. Among Black people in the United States, however, a marriage may endure partly because of support by family members, but also because the mates are well-suited and have a good "understanding," including social, psychological, and economic arrangements. In either case, the marital tie does not enjoy quite the central and absolute status it generally holds among middle-class Whites, who create a socially and economically independent family unit.

My work in Chicago suggested that the Black family is extended in character, often showing a bilateral tendency, but more frequently oriented toward the maternal side in the families I studied. A household may include members beyond the nuclear family—one or more grandparents, cousins, aunts, nieces, or nephews. When sons and daughters marry, they usually leave home, but they often remain in the same neighborhood as their parents and form closely-knit groups. In some cases, the newlywed couple may move to other cities where relatives are settled. These localized family groups are the focus of childrearing; they are an economic boon to working parents and are the agents of socializing the young. Children learn a variety of social roles and values within this extended group.

As evident in the material presented in the following pages, men play a variety of roles and role types in Black families; they may be good providers (father or husband), family leaders (maternal or paternal uncle), sources of rivalry and support (brother), or focuses of pride or concern (son or nephew). One individual does not necessarily exemplify all of these role types during his lifetime. A widower or bachelor without children of his own may concentrate on keeping the larger family group together; a devoted husband and father may lose touch with his own relatives; or a man may never fully settle into any of the adult family roles, thereby remaining the prodigal son or younger brother throughout his lifetime. Within one extended group, however, the total range of kinship roles is generally present, with a wide variation in their performance. The child is exposed to a spectrum of activities and values of men that may be represented, on the one hand, by the apparently solitary, free-floating male, and on the other, by the pillar of the community, both of whom play a part in his socialization. Male family members reflect a variety of values and life possibilities; they serve as a foil to the women, who represent the necessarily circumscribed business of procreation and social continuity. The perennial conflict between these contradictory, yet complementary, functions creates the dynamics of the man-woman relationship. Thus, the Black child learns about the many facets of his society, and its values are transmitted to him from within his kin group, which is not limited to the conjugal family of parents and children.

One might conclude from this and other studies of Black family life that the relationships between men and women are highly competitive and that there is a great deal of sexual separatism as a result of economic competition. It is true that Black women may earn as much or more than Black men (though they usually earn less) and that conflict frequently centers around finances. Also, the care and support of children is more directly the concern of women than men. The deeper level, upon which there is profound agreement and cooperation, should not be overlooked, however, nor should the strength of family ties that draw men as fathers, brothers, and uncles, to children. Although men may not support children as a matter of course, they are generous when asked for help.

The men and women described in these pages agree on the supreme importance of a love relationship between a man and a woman and on the necessity of caring and bringing up properly any offspring resulting from their union. Their disagreements stem from the means employed in expressing those values and, as in most relationships, a power struggle ensues. Even here, men and women know the terms of the struggle; and are able to communicate clearly with each other. Still, the conditions of the settlement are not known in advance, but are the outcome of a series of negotiations which must be reasonably acceptable to both parties. If all the ingredients for a successful relationship are present, it is only a matter of time to work it out. Otherwise, there are few external pressures holding a man and woman together.

Another role relationship in the Black family that may be misinterpreted by an observer with a White, middle-class background is that of mother and daughter. The relationship between a woman and her grown daughter counterbalances, and may conflict with, that between a man and a woman. In the absence of a husband and father, mother and daughter are made strongly interdependent by children born to either of them. Being a mother is a highly valued role in Black communities, as is characteristic of many societies in which recruitment to the socially important group is by birth. With motherhood comes responsibility, and shared responsibility brings adults together. A mother may not encourage her daughter to marry, since she will lose her support and a measure of domestic authority. A daughter may be looking for a father for her children, but will wait until she finds a good provider; in the meantime, her dependence on her mother may keep her from forming an attachment with a man. Most women choose to marry at some time in their lives, but if a marriage does not work, often a woman can turn to her mother or other family members for help.

Children brought up in the Black families I have come to know have an intimate knowledge of a wide range of social relationships, and experience a complexity of attitudes and values that are not encountered by children in the conjugal family setting. I would venture to infer from my association with them and from my knowledge of their family backgrounds that they develop a profound understanding of social situations and a strong social identity at a comparatively early age. Discussion and explanation of rules of social behavior occurred persistently within the

Black families I observed, and everyone supported his own firm opinion with arguments. Discipline is often strict and concerned with teaching children to show respect to their elders and to adult authority in general. The continuous assertion and contest of wills on the part of adults in Black families encourages the development of strong-willed individuals who, nevertheless, will give respect when it is due.

How did I, as a White female from a middle-class background, become aware of my original mistaken assumptions about the Black family and come to test them? With some experience of the essential dependence of the outside observer, I put my informants in the role of tutors: I made a decision early in my investigation to concentrate on a few people and to come to know them well, rather than to try to include a large number of families in my study. Most of those I contacted were friendly and open, and some of them became friends. My interviews with the latter were two-way exchanges of experiences, feelings, and ideas. By opening my own actions and ideas to comments from Black friends, I was apprised of differences in our respective viewpoints, and through our mutual friendships I gained an insight into the meaning of experiences to them. While my viewpoint, as modified by these experiences, is not and never can be identical to that of someone who has grown up and lived in a Black community, perhaps it carries a certain validity as an "outsider's view" with a degree of understanding of what it means to be Black. We need studies of Black communities by Black as well as White social scientists and studies of White communities by both Black and White investigators in order to gain a complete perspective on these major divisions within our society.

Discussions about the participant-observer and case study methods have focused on the validity of nonquantitative data and the reliability and significance of observations based on a small sample. In my view, these concerns are misplaced, since the role of participant observation and the case study is not primarily to test hypotheses, but to question and challenge assumptions on which hypotheses are based. It may be that an investigator asks the wrong or least penetrating questions because his or her assumptions are based on participant observation in his own social milieu; the intensive interaction of participant observation in a new setting opens the investigator to experiences upon which further hypotheses can be based and about which different questions can be asked. For example, countless quantitative data concerning illegitimacy, matrifocal households, and the weakness of the conjugal tie in Black families have been collected to test hypotheses about masculine identification, the social and cultural deprivation of Black children, and the consequences of the disorganization of Black family life, based on a conjugal-family model. Through my interaction in a number of Black households, I became aware of situations that could not be explained or understood on the basis of old assumptions about the Black family as a more or less "successful" reflection of a "dominant" American family type. In explaining and interpreting a few cases, I began to look more carefully at data whose significance had been overlooked—such as the relative strength of parent-child and sibling ties—and a new perspective developed out of this, according to which family strength is measured by considerations other than marital stability or illegitimacy. Based on these new assumptions, hypotheses can be developed, namely, concerning the sources of ego strength of Black men in a female-headed household and the bases of household organization other than economic deprivation. Such hypotheses can be tested and generalizations formed by comparing with previous studies, looking for corroborating data whose significance may have been overlooked previously, and by generating new studies.

As has emerged from the case material in this study, Black family organization differs from White, middle-class family organization in that consanguineal relationships are frequently emphasized as much as or more than the conjugal tie. I have used the term "extended family," which has been widely applied by anthropologists in the study of other societies, to describe the Black family. Some writers have been cognizant of strong ties among Black kindred; they have focused on the makeup of households and on kinship networks as adaptive strategies, using concepts such as "matrifocality" and "personal kindred" to characterize them.[4] The Black family is viewed by these writers as essentially an adjustment to urban ghetto conditions, rather than as a continuing institution. The emphasis on household organization and on adaptation results in overlooking important aspects of family organization and structure, such as the maintenance of family ties through space and time by means of conscious and ritualized practices in funerals, reunions, and regular visiting patterns. Chapters 1 and 6 of this study emphasize this aspect of Black families, as do other descriptions of families throughout the text.

A comparison of my conclusions with those of studies of Southern and Caribbean families reveals similarities that support the view of the Black family as a cultural institution with a long tradition, rather than an adaptation to specific conditions. In a study of American slavery, George P. Rawick presents evidence for the existence of a strong kinship group among black slaves, as well as for the conscious maintenance of other African cultural patterns.[5] In British Guiana, and among the Black Carib, consanguineal ties are strong, and economic and social support among kin are the rule.[6] In her article, "Family and Childhood in a Southern Negro Community," Virginia Heyer Young stresses the functional and systematic aspects of the Black family, in which grandparents play an important role.[7] Family activities and the influence of a wide group of kin remain strong in the memories of my Chicago contacts from the South. From his comparative study of Black families in Chicago and Black families from the Caribbean, Raymond T. Smith concludes that in neither case is the nuclear family the norm, but rather it is an extended kin group.[8]

The way one interprets the same data, either as evidence for a continuing tradition or as confirmation of the view that the Black family represents an adaptation of a middle-class norm to conditions of poverty, depends upon one's own orientation: whether or not one accepts the idea of a Black culture within American

[4] Cf. Nancie L. Gonzalez, "Toward a Definition of Matrifocality"; and Carol B. Stack, "The Kindred of Viola Jackson: Residence and Family Organization of an Urban Black American Family," in Norman E. Whitten, Jr. and John F. Szwed, eds., *Afro-American Anthropology*. New York: Crowell-Collier-Macmillan, 1970.

[5] George P. Rawick, *The American Slave: A Composite Autobiography*. Vol. 1: From Sundown to Sunup: The Making of the Black Community. New York: Greenwood Publishing Co., 1972.

[6] See footnotes 3 and 4.

[7] Virginia Heyer Young, "Family and Childhood in a Southern Negro Community," *American Anthropologist*, vol. 72, no. 2, April 1970, pp. 269–288.

[8] Raymond T. Smith, "The Nuclear Family in Afro-American Kinship," *Journal of Comparative Family Studies*, vol. 1, no. 1, 1970, pp. 55–70.

society, which was created out of many diverse elements from the past and the present. In his article, "Black Culture, Myth or Reality," Robert Blauner presents a strong case for such a view.[9] While working among young Black people, I have observed the development of new social perceptions and conscious creative efforts, both social and artistic; such activities generally accompany cultural innovation and the modification of a tradition. The regularities and ritual aspects of Black social organization, may be obscured by terms such as "adaptive strategy" and "adaptive subculture," which imply strategies for survival. In Chapter 7, the concept of adaptation is viewed from the perspective of the rational choice according to cultural values and alternatives, rather than in instrumental terms only.

The "culture of poverty," an essentially negative concept, is also insufficient: surely mere poverty cannot account for the richness and variety in the Black cultural tradition.[10] The strength of Black people stems from a social organization that has been created in the face of adversity, and not merely in adjustment to it. Blacks have neither passively endured poverty nor made it a virtue or a basis for their lives.

Among the families in these pages are those that are or have been relatively affluent, and others that have known only poverty. While class differences are represented here, I have stressed the values and concepts that they share while attempting to give due recognition to individual differences and variation in social patterns. Despite differences in opinions and value conflicts, I have found similar themes in the lives of friends and informants. On the basis of these observations, I have opted for a view of the "Black experience" as a complex phenomenon in a heterogeneous society, creating in many ways a unique way of life for Black men and women in our society.

In presenting my findings about Black families in Chicago, I have relied on life histories and on the presentation of "social drama," described by V. W. Turner as "a limited area of transparency on the otherwise opaque surface of regular, uneventful social life."[11] He regards the depiction of dramatic events as of utmost importance in the study of social organization: "Through it we are enabled to observe the crucial principles of the social structure in their operation, and their relative dominance at different points of time."[12] Frankenberg[13] characterizes social drama as the prime contribution of anthropology to the study of complex societies. The participant-observer records the face-to-face encounters present in all societies, whether complex or simple; by observing and analyzing crisis events, ceremonials, and daily encounters between individuals the anthropologist is describing social process, leading to a dynamic view of social organization. Accordingly,

[9] In Norman E. Whitten, Jr. and John F. Szwed, eds., *Afro-American Anthropology*. New York: Crowell-Collier-Macmillan, 1970.
[10] Cf. Charles A. Valentine, *Culture and Poverty, Critique and Counter-Proposals*. Chicago: University of Chicago Press, 1968.
[11] V. W. Turner, *Schism and Continuity in an African Society*. Manchester, Eng.: Manchester University Press, 1957, p. 93.
[12] *Ibid.*
[13] Ronald Frankenberg, "British Community Studies: Problems of Synthesis," in Michael Banton, ed., *The Social Anthropology of Complex Societies*. ASA Monographs 4. London: Tavistock Publications, Ltd., 1966.

this treatment is not written so that one can skip over details and concentrate on generalizations; rather, the technique is to build up a mosaic of social reality through the juxtaposition of life experiences, in an attempt to convey a complexity that cannot be grasped through the bald statement of fact or theory.

Social organization in Black communities is undergoing increasing change; in Chapter 7 I have attempted to place the intensive Chicago study in historical perspective, as well as to compare my findings with those of other studies of the Black family. For the most part, however, the material presented is based on a social reality limited in time and space, and viewed from the perspective of both a profound and personal experience.[14]

[14] My study was part of a larger project administered by the Center for Urban Studies at the University of Chicago and directed by David M. Schneider and Raymond T. Smith. The study was financed by a grant by the Children's Bureau of the Department of Health, Education and Welfare of the U. S. Government (Grant No. R328). I would like to thank these agencies and individuals for making the study possible; however, they are not responsible for the ideas and opinions expressed in the present work.

1 / Lifeline

INTRODUCTION

Since their African ancestors were transported from their homes and lands to a foreign shore, Black Americans have periodically experienced separation from their families and friends, and have known the intense loneliness of rejection. Before the Emancipation Proclamation, the journey to freedom meant that families and friendships would be split apart. As Frederick Douglass informs us, some found this too great a price to pay and chose to remain in bondage rather than leave their circle of intimates.

Inheriting and passing on a tradition of indomitable feminine strength, Harriet Tubman stands out as one who with determination led her people toward freedom and helped to weave the fabric of relationships among Blacks in the North. Following the leadership of Frederick Douglass, Harriet Tubman, and other great historical figures, Black Americans have displayed in their kinship organization a capacity for individual mobility and freedom with security that has enabled generations of Black Americans to "try their luck" in a new environment.

The Southern heritage was not forgotten. The warmth and familiarity of small town and rural Southern life was aspired to but never quite attained in Northern ghettos. But here and there, individuals freed from traditional constraints penetrated the White world in the North, bringing recognition of a way of life forged by descendants of those among America's earliest settlers.

FREEDOM TRAIN TO CHICAGO

A New Beginning When she was twenty-three, a "grown woman" with an adventurous spirit, Lucille Foster left her home in Hattiesburg, Mississippi, and moved to Chicago. Her marriage was in crisis. Her husband, feeling trapped between his aspirations and his frustrations, had deserted her when she was pregnant; he then returned only to beat her and to lock her up at home when he felt threatened by her independent ways. Lucille tolerated this treatment for only a few months. One day, while he was at work, she withdrew her savings from a secret account she had opened before her marriage, bought a train ticket, and departed for Chicago with her eight-month-old son.

9

Leaving for Chicago

Lucille was aware of the numerous migrations made by her people, throughout their history, to loneliness and an alien way of life; still, fragments of conversation and childhood ambitions pulled her on to the North and to the city. She left her family—her mother, father, sisters, and brothers—in Hattiesburg, as well as other relatives on her mother's side. However, she also had relatives living in Detroit, Chicago, and California, who occasionally returned to Mississippi for visits. Lucille could stay with any of them until she was settled, a possibility that would mitigate the strangeness of her new situation. She especially wanted to see her favorite aunt, Lucille, after whom she was named. But Aunt Lucille lived in Los Angeles, which was much too far away. She would not be able to come back home if she wanted to or was needed, an alternative that provided her with further insurance against loneliness. So she decided on Chicago. With baggage and baby, she appeared at her Aunt Louise's home on the South Side, creating a mild shock. They were not happy to see her, but she was there, with nowhere else to go. And Aunt Louise had experienced the indifference of the city to newcomers.

When she left Hattiesburg, Lucille realized that her husband would eventually follow her to Chicago. After a month or so he arrived and found a job; they remained together for awhile, then separated. It was not any one thing that brought about the final breakup, Lucille explained later, just a number of the things that happen to Black men and women. When Lucille started working, Foster wanted her to pay half the rent and to split the other bills. She decided then to make it on her own and to live her life as she wanted. So she left again, this time permanently.

Lucille had been working as a nurse's aide; now she elected to go into training as a practical nurse. She moved back to her aunt's home, but her aunt's husband caused so much trouble that she had to leave. While Louise felt an obligation to her sister's daughter, her husband did not, and she allowed herself to be influenced by a man who cared little for family ties, and certainly not for those of his wife. Lucille had to find another place to stay.

Where would she turn? She had no money, no job, and a one-year-old son. She had recently made some friends, but which of them would be willing to take on such a burden? Then "Aunt Peach," an energetic old lady from "down home" came to the rescue; she was visiting some friends who agreed to take care of Lucille and her son. As arranged, Lucille would pay them when she started working. As soon as she had completed her training and began her career as a practical nurse, Lucille got an apartment of her own. She was independent at last!

The Extension of Kinship   Relatives and close friends, what would one do without them? Back home, most of Lucille's mother's family lived right up the street or, at most, a half-hour away by shortcut, in the little town of Flower, Mississippi. Lucille's grandmother and some of her cousins lived in Flower, and she and her sister used to go there often on Sundays, where they attended church and Young People's Union. While they were growing up, their playmates were their cousins; not until she was in high school did Lucille make friends outside her family.

Besides Lucille's real relatives, there had been those old people who were always "just there." If you know anything about the South, you have heard about the custom of calling someone "Aunt" or "Uncle" even though they are not related. Years later, Lucille still recalls "Uncle Honey," who warmed himself by their fire in the evenings, and a lot of others whose exact relationship—or whether there was one—she does not know. Two "cousins," Frank and Tom, live in Chicago. Lucille does not know how they got to be cousins, but their mother is "Aunt Peach," who may be a great aunt—"or something."

While one may call people who are unrelated "Aunt" or "Uncle" in the South, one may or may not consider a real aunt's or uncle's spouse as kin. Marriage is problematic: it is the day-to-day contact or concern and help that count when one is thinking of family beyond "blood" relatives. Lucille did not consider Louise's first husband as an uncle; when Louise married Freddy, a man who appreciates the importance of family, the situation changed. Freddy cut her son's hair, and he encouraged Louise to visit her family in Mississippi every year when he visited his family in Georgia. To Lucille he is "Uncle Freddy."

"Aunt Lily," who lives in Chicago, is married to Lucille's mother's cousin. Lucille likes Aunt Lily, or Miss Lily, as she often calls her, and feels Miss Lily was badly treated by Cousin Garfield. Miss Lily is older than Garfield—only two years older, "although," says Lucille, "the way they used to talk about it, I thought it must have been at least twenty-five years!" In the South, you should marry someone close to your own age. And the woman should never be older—not even by as much as a month! Lucille used to go to Miss Lily's house in the morning, after working the nightshift, and Miss Lily would prepare a huge breakfast. She does not go over as often now, since Miss Lily is living with her daughter, Delores, who constantly fights with her husband. Aunt Lily lives upstairs and Delores and her family live on the ground floor.

Occasionally, when Lucille visits Miss Lily, she stops in to talk to Delores, too. On one visit, Delores was nursing a black eye and a grudge against her husband, which she justified in convincing detail. But while Lucille was there, Delores' husband called and it appeared that all was forgotten. He announced that he was going to Detroit for the weekend and Delores decided to go with him, although it meant missing her son's graduation from grammar school. "He'll spend all his money, so I might as well go along," she explained. Lucille, who had offered to alter the boy's graduation suit, disapproved of such irresponsibility. Delores was far too much under the influence of her husband if she neglected her children like that! Still, despite her critical view of Delores' life style, Lucille considers her a cousin, though the relationship is distant. Along with kinship goes moral responsibility, but Lucille is not one to condemn.

Southern folk do not limit their circle of kin to real or assumed relatives. They add "play mothers and fathers" and "play sisters and brothers" onto an already full set of kin. A woman without children or whose children have left home might "take on" a play daughter. She will act like a mother to her or, at least in some ways, will play the part of mother. She will buy her play daughter gifts—usually clothing—at birthdays and at Christmas. The girl will play the part of "daughter" by going to the store for her or doing some light housework, nothing too strenuous. Sometimes she may even stay overnight.

Lucille remembers her two play mothers with warmth. While she was staying with relatives in Alabama one year, her principal's wife looked after her and bought her an outfit for the Homecoming Dance. Her other play mother was a former neighbor in Hattiesburg. Lucille's youngest sister, Flo, is named after her. She now lives in Los Angeles and keeps in touch with Aunt Lucille, who also lives there. Lucille would like to see both of them sometime—her play mother must be really old by now!

When closest bonds are with family, what better way to show friendship than by extending family relationships? And what better way to bridge the generations? One can become agreeably involved, with the option of limiting the involvement. For instance, Lucille was concerned when a high school girl in Hattiesburg who calls herself Lucille's play daughter, became pregnant by a much older man. The same man had tried to date Lucille when she was home one summer. Afterward, she heard the gossip about her play daughter and was naturally upset, but she did not feel obliged to do anything about it. She could even laugh a little about the old entrepreneur.

There may be a number of reasons, both economic and sentimental, to set up a play relationship with someone. Earline, a real sister of Lucille's play sister, came to live with Lucille's family when she was in her teens. Earline's parents had given up on her, calling her the "black sheep," and Lucille's mother, a close neighbor, brought her up. Earline was not really a play sister, but more like an adopted sister. She and Dora Lee, Lucille's eldest sister, became inseparable, and Lucille felt left out. To make up for it, she entered into a play relationship with Earline's sister, creating, so to speak, a "balance of power."

Lucille still keeps in touch with her play sister, who, along with Earline and other members of her family, has since moved to Chicago. Earline says that she herself does not associate much with her own, real family, and speaks of Lucille's mother and father and Dora Lee and her children as "my family." She also claims that she would send them money and do other things for them sooner than she would for her own people. Earline is godmother for Dora Lee's grandchild, having sent clothes and money for the christening, and every time Dora Lee visits, Earline sends back clothing for her "nieces and nephews."

Whenever Dora Lee comes North to visit Lucille she spends time with Earline as well. Lucille and Earline meet only when Dora Lee is there. Both are strong-willed, outspoken women, who are frequently antagonistic toward each other. Often Earline expresses her worries about Dora Lee, who, she feels, is far too good-natured (she passively allows her husband to continue his involvement with another woman). Lucille defends her sister by saying that her husband's "fooling around" leaves Dora Lee free for affairs of her own and, as long as he continues to support her children, Dora Lee is "doing all right!" She further points out that Earline, with a son whom she must periodically bail out of jail, should not be feeling sorry for others. Generally, however, out of consideration for her sister, Lucille is circumspect in what she says to Earline.

Throughout her childhood and early youth, Lucille was surrounded by a network of family as well as friends of the family. She has attempted to recreate that environment in Chicago, emphasizing family ties and close friendships, even when it conflicts with material gain in the form of luxuries or personal advancement. Lucille has made many friends in Chicago. She is open and generous, though often sarcastic about human failings. She reserves her most biting sarcasm for men, most of whom she feels "aren't ready" (which refers to anything from marriage to "liberation"), although she has many male friends. Her closest girlfriend, Donna, was a practical nurse when they met, but she now works in an office. Donna, a quiet, fragile-appearing woman, found the work as a Licensed Practical Nurse (LPN) far too difficult; she likes ease and luxury. Her elegant apartment contrasts with Lucille's rather plain, unadorned flat. She and Lucille are about the same age, and they are both single with unhappy marriages behind them. They keep up on each other's love affairs and give each other advice that often goes unheeded.

When Donna and Lucille vacationed together in the Bahamas, Donna was "too scared to have a good time," Lucille reported afterwards. Lucille had met the most attractive men, while Donna stayed locked in her room. She raved about the men and the good time she had had, and teased Donna about being so timid. Donna said little, but the following year she went back to the Bahamas with another friend and this time, she said pointedly, she had had a ball!

Donna's parents are like father and mother to Lucille. She used to rent an apartment from them and they took care of her son when he was a baby. Later on, after she had moved to new quarters, a fire broke out, which destroyed a living room set she had just purchased and most of her clothing. Desperate, she called Donna's parents, and they came to assist her within fifteen minutes. When Donna's stepfather died, Lucille said she felt it was almost as though her own father had died. She attended the funeral as a member of the family, riding along with them in the limousine. She became quite emotional during the funeral service.

All of Lucille's "blood relatives," adopted relatives, "play" relatives and friends have helped her to make her way in Chicago. But there is an important difference between Aunt Louise—her mother's sister—and "Aunt" Lily, Donna's parents, and her other adopted relatives. Although she and Aunt Louise have differences, they are very much concerned about each other. After Lucille left Aunt Louise's home, she still stopped by every Sunday after work, at which time her aunt would prepare a big Sunday dinner. This was reminiscent of old times in Mississippi, when they all went to Lucille's grandmother's house on Sundays. Aunt Louise also babysat for Lucille when Robert was a baby. They see each other often, sometimes two or three times a week, meeting at Aunt Louise's house or downtown; Aunt Louise comes to Lucille's apartment only when her sister, Lucille's mother, is up from Mississippi.

Family "Outposts"   Louise's Aunt Sarah—Lucille's great-aunt and Miss Lily's mother-in-law—was the first of Lucille's relatives to move to Chicago. She came after her children were grown, but they followed later: Garfield with his wife, Lily, and his sister. Aunt Louise arrived next and stayed with Aunt Sarah until she was settled. Then came Lucille, who stayed with Louise. A few years later, Lucille's eldest brother, Terry, came North and lived with her for awhile. He was supposed to finish school, but she found out that he was gambling with the money she gave him for lunch and carfare, so she turned him out. "Big city life seemed to get to those small-town Southern boys!" she reflects. Terry's uncle in Detroit, a high school principal, offered to put him through school, but he did not like Detroit and was soon back in his Chicago circuit. He finally got a permanent job in factory, but he could never seem to settle his personal affairs: every time Lucille saw him he would introduce a new girlfriend whom he was "going to marry." He and Lucille see each other only occasionally now, and when they do, they have little to say to each other.

A couple of years after Terry's arrival, Aunt Rose's eldest daughter came from Mississippi to stay with Lucille, but Lucille sent her home after a few months. She was too independent for an eighteen-year-old, Lucille felt, and she feared she would get into trouble. She went back home to Mississippi for a year, then married a man from New York and moved there. Later, her brother and sister also moved to New York. In several key Northern cities—New York, Chicago, Detroit, Los Angeles—Lucille has relatives who will take in ambitious young family members until they are able to fend for themselves.

Lucille's family contrasts with Earline's: Earline's mother, father, brothers, and sisters all moved to Chicago together. She has no people in Mississippi besides Lucille's family. In other families, one or two sisters or brothers started the move and the others followed, all of them congregating in the same area of Chicago. In Lucille's family, the basic "lifeline," as she calls it, has extended through the generations, with those in one generation helping those in the next to settle in a new situation. But in each generation, a contingent of family members remains in Mississippi, giving the family a firm Southern base. They own land which, as poor as it may be, gives the family a certain stake in the society.

Also, Lucille's family tends toward the female line. Men are involved primarily as brothers, sons, uncles, and nephews; as husbands and fathers they play important, but less defined, roles that are subject to negotiation. They take over where the "family" leaves off. If they fail in their roles, the family, including uncles and brothers as well as mothers, sisters, and aunts, remains as a continuing support.

Among her brothers and sisters, Lucille is closest to Dora Lee, who visits her every summer. Every year she promises to stay in Chicago, but she is always ready to return home even sooner than she planned. Her eldest son calls up to complain about what a bad time they are having without her, and that ends her visit. To Lucille's disappointment, she is off to Mississippi within the week.

Terry still lives in Chicago, but he is nearly invisible as far as Lucille is concerned. On the other hand, Dora Lee is close to Terry; she understands Lucille's anger toward him, but she is more sympathetic. On her last visit to Chicago, she announced that she was determined to see Terry at all costs. For one thing, their parents had given her a message for him, and besides, she wanted to see her brother. She went to the taverns that Lucille said he frequented and left word for him, although his cronies denied any knowledge of him. At last, having received the message through some circuitous route known only to himself, Terry appeared at Lucille's home and they all went out for the evening. The next day he took Dora Lee's little daughter and Lucille's son to the beach. This was a substantial bit of family life for Terry, who, at the time, had not seen Lucille for over six months, and had been back home only once since he left, nearly 15 years before. His sisters advised him to go home to see his parents, but it was just too hard for him to go home. He feels that no one could understand.

Another brother, Harlow, lives in Wisconsin. He calls Lucille occasionally, at her expense, and comes to see Terry whenever he gets a chance; they, too, are very close. At home, Harlow had joined the Freedom Riders, although his parents did not like the idea. Once he asked them whether they would bail him out if he were put in jail. They said they would not and were upset when he replied, "That's all right, I'm not doing anything in school, anyway. I might just as well be in jail." At one point, he refused to speak to them when he met them on the street, but they understood—he did not want it to be known that they were related, for fear that they might be harmed.

Harlow came North with one of the Freedom Riders and lived with his family— a White family—while finishing high school. He lived in a small town where some of the children had never seen a Black person. They used to come close to him just to get a good look at him and to touch him. He learned how to get along with White people and became popular at school. His classmates loved it when he began to dance and "cut up." He grew an Afro, wore a dashiki, and learned how to play Bongo drums. He went on to college in Wisconsin, where he employed his talents as an entertainer to some advantage, but he missed his family and went back home whenever he could.

Out of six brothers and sisters in Lucille's generation, three—the eldest and youngest girls and the youngest boy—seem to be settled in Hattiesburg. They have no objection to moving up North, or to a city, but on the other hand, they apparently have no overwhelming desire to leave home. They probably feel that things would be no better elsewhere. Many of Lucille's relatives and family friends have gone North, only to return disappointed. Those who, like Lucille, have a restless urge to move ahead can adjust to the faster pace of Northern city life.

MISSISSIPPI CHILD

Southern Roots   Lucille is fairly satisfied with her life in Chicago; still, within the sophisticated city woman persists a generous measure of the Southern small town girl. Whenever Dora Lee comes North for a visit there is an air of excitement, of past shared experiences and feelings, for the two sisters are very close. They reminisce about old times and Dora Lee's wide, friendly face gleams with humor; tactfully she backs up Lucille's sudden rather sporadic thrusts into the past. It emerges that Lucille was a quiet, serious child, who read all the time while others were having fun. Dora Lee says they all thought she would be an old maid. Their father, who did not believe much in education, said she would not amount to anything because she was always "using her head." She would not go out and pick cotton like the rest of them, but took jobs helping out various ladies in town.

Lucille used to be active in church; she played the piano and sang in the choir. She took piano lessons, mainly because Earline's sister, her "play sister," did and she wanted to do everything everyone else did. Her mother paid for the lessons, but her parents never bought her the piano they promised. She had to practice at her teacher's house and the old lady would yell at her whenever she made a mistake.

Lucille's motto was, "Everything you can do, I can do better." She was a part of everything at school—plays, musical activities, even 4H—although she never lived on a farm. In the seventh grade she played the leading lady in "Snow White and the Seven Dwarfs." Lucille was always right at the center of all the action, at least that's the way it was at school. Whenever they had to raise money for anything, she did as much or more than anyone. She recalls, "those awful salmon sandwiches they used to make and sell at the end-of-the-year program, with chopped egg, onion, and pickle!" She could not even look at one of them now!

Even as a child, Dora Lee was a sharp contrast to Lucille. She was a true Mississippi Black belle—plump, with fat braids. Lucille was scrawny, with short red hair. Their mother always took Dora Lee with her wherever she went, because she was proud of her, but she left Lucille at home. When Lucille was older she made new outfits for herself frequently and went to have her picture taken in her new clothes. The photographer told her she was very photogenic and tried to persuade her to travel with him. But it was not until much later that she realized the advantage of being slim.

Growing Pains   When the two girls were children, they were not allowed to play with boys. They played house with their cousins, baking mud cakes, catching and cooking cray fish and grass, and even real greens. They sometimes stole grease and really cooked. They built houses under the high front porch with rooms

Childhood in Mississippi

out of cardboard. The boys stayed away—they knew they were not allowed to be near the girls.

Later on, it was different. Dora Lee used to sneak out to meet her girlfriends and boyfriends. Lucille did not have much to do with boys; she did not like most of the boys in her class and only spoke to one or two occasionally. Once Dora Lee and her friend persuaded Lucille to come along with them on a date. They employed the ruse of telling their mother that there was a party and that Sally's mother had said she could go if they could; then they told Sally's mother the same thing. In this way they got away, and the older two joined their boyfriends. Lucille's date had to take his girlfriend home first, but as Lucille remembers it, he was so anxious to join them that he did not even take his girlfriend all the way home. "That's men for you!" she concludes philosophically.

They went to a place where there was dancing and the first so-called "television" in the area. Actually, it was more like a juke box that showed pictures of the performing artists. Louis Jordan and his Strings were popular at the time, Lucille recalls. Lucille refused to go in, since she was afraid of what her mother might say, so they drove on to an area where Blacks and Whites who were married to each other lived. It was dangerous: those people would not tolerate anyone trespassing in their territory. The other couples started kissing and petting, and Lucille heard Dora Lee's friend say "I will if she will." Lucille hit the boy who was supposed to be with her when he tried to kiss her. She did not like him anyway; he was not even in school. Just then, they heard gunshots and decided they had better leave. They were so frightened that they drove too fast and the car turned over. No one was hurt, but they got dust all over their Sunday clothes. They did not even have money to take the bus home. Finally, an old White man came along and transported them to the bus line and gave them money to take the bus. Lucille was embarrassed when she saw a boy she knew and liked at school on the bus; she hated being seen in her bedraggled and dirty condition.

When they got home, their mother was waiting for them, but their father would not let her touch them. He said, "Remember, when you were that age you ran away from home and got married." But they had to come straight home from school for a month afterward and could not go anywhere in the evenings. Ruining their best clothes was a most serious offense!

Lucille's childhood was shaped by rules and sobered by punishment and humiliation. Still, she came to know the lighter and more pleasant side of life as well, primarily through her father.

Lucille idolized her father; if he was there, he would not allow their mother or grandmother to lay a hand on them. His nickname was "Tang," and people would say, "Don't touch those little old Tang children 'cause they Daddy get you." He was their defense. Their mother was strict. She used to braid switches from straps of an old trunk and keep them ready. Sometimes, when there was a fire, they would say to their father, "Here's mother's strap—why don't you burn it?" And he would pitch it into the fire. He could be a devil that way sometimes.

Lucille's mother was their boss and disciplinarian. Even if it was a week later, she would punish them for doing something they should not have done. Lucille recalls getting most of the whippings. Her mother reasoned. "It couldn't have been Dora Lee, she is older and knows better." Lucille became a "fighter"; she and Dora Lee slept in the same bed and they argued over the covers or about who touched whom. That is the only time her father ever hit her—when she fought with her sister.

Lucille was so angered at receiving so many beatings that she often said, "When I get away from here I'll never come back." After she moved to Chicago, however, her husband had to lock her in her room to keep her from going back to Mississippi every month.

After so many beatings, Lucille grew so concerned about what her mother said and thought, that she began to squeal on the others. Their neighbor, one of Dora Lee's boyfriends ran away from home about twice a week. Once Lucille's father, who always noticed when anything was out of place, complained that someone had been in his smokehouse. Lucille had seen the boy sneaking out of the smokehouse that day; he had been staying there. He offered her pop and potato chips in return for her silence. She accepted the bribe, then told anyway, at least indirectly. She always told, in one way or another.

His Children's Daddy Lucille's father put his children first, even ahead of his wife. Whenever they went to his place of work they would give a special whistle and he would stop whatever he was doing, no matter who he was talking to, and say, "My children are here; I'll have to see what they want." Whenever he asked one of them to do something for him, they would go to great lengths to do it, while their mother would have to ask them ten times. He gave them spending money and brought them something when he came home, even if it was only a big apple. He would peel it, slice it into little bits, and feed it to them, piece by piece. His children always had food to eat and clothes on their back. Even during the long depression he made certain that everyone, including neighbors, had enough to eat from his hunting and fishing. He caught big catfish, so big their intestines were dripping with fat, and sold them for a quarter apiece. He also smoked pork for his family and for the neighbors, who gave him neckbones, entrails, and feet in return. The younger children cannot appreciate their father because they do not know him when he was younger and more active. When he had not been well for a long time, they seemed to regard him as an irritating old man, who was not entitled to much respect. This hurt Lucille, who was very close to her father. She used to go fishing with him and tagged along wherever he went. He had always wanted a son, of course, and Terry, Jr. came along when she was nine. She was very jealous of Terry and would pinch him when she changed his diapers. She felt that she had been supplanted.

Lucille never liked her maternal grandmother very much, because she knew she had been opposed to her mother's marriage to her father. She could also be mean sometimes. Every week they had to go over to her house to wash her clothes, pound them and put them into scalding water with lye, twice over. They would take peaches from her tree and play on her porch, while she watched them through the windows. Occasionally she would come out and hit them. Lucille's grandfather had been a deacon in the church and all she remembers about him is that he sat out on the porch, each evening in the dark, eating his dinner. He died suddenly one night in his sleep.

Her grandmother had been against the marriage between Lucille's mother, Aretha, and her father, because Aretha was only fifteen or sixteen and Lucille's father had already been married once before and had a son Aretha's age. Since Lucille was a little girl she heard the story of how her parents had finally gotten married. Aunt Lucille, Aretha's sister, and her husband had engineered it. The three went shopping one day with their mother. The lights in the store went out and, when they came back on, Aretha and Aunt Lucille's husband had gone, thus leaving Aunt Lucille to handle her mother. Aretha and her brother-in-law met Lucille's father and they went on to the justice of the peace, where the marriage ceremony was held.

When he moved to Hattiesburg, Lucille's father was a railroad man, traveling cross-country. He decided to settle down for awhile in Hattiesburg; he lived a few houses down from Aunt Lucille. When Aretha came in from Flower to visit her sister, the two met, and have been together ever since. Her father sometimes jokes about the "black woman" he married, for Aretha is very dark. "Here I am, married to a 'black woman,' " he says, "and I've always been afraid of 'black women.' " Lucille's mother remains silent when he teases like that. Once Lucille asked her mother how she was able to contend with her father's drinking, fooling, and teasing all those years. Her mother had answered, "When you're older, you'll understand. It means a lot to have someone who will stand by you and take care of your children." Lucille does understand now, but she has never found a man like her father.

Lucille has pleasant memories of her father's mother, long dead now. She was a sweet lady with a rust-colored face and long, black hair. She had a lot of Indian blood. Her husband deserted her when their children were young; they all grew up, married, and lived in Castlewood, Alabama, with the exception of Lucille's father. Lucille's family used to visit her father's mother every year at Christmas, and her father gave his mother a one-hundred dollar bill as a present. Even later, after they stopped visiting every year, he sent her fifty or one hundred dollars.

They all enjoyed the visits to Alabama. People would come in to see them and Lucille's father would show off his children, who were called "Little Tang." His youngest sister, "Baby," always made a black walnut cake for him and would say, "I made your favorite cake, brother," and Lucille's father would always eat it. It was so heavy and sticky, though, that Lucille could never eat her piece. "Baby" did not keep herself or her kitchen very clean, Lucille recalls, and she once saw her mother sneak out at night and throw away her piece, too.

The "Coming Out"   After Terry was born, the family stopped going to Alabama every year. One year Lucille spent the summer there and then stayed on for the school year. She stayed with her father's son by his first wife, who had two children. Lula Bell, his daughter, was about Lucille's age. The two girls got along very well. They both were quiet and serious. They had a good time that year. Lucille held prestige, being from the "city," and they could attract the attention of certain boys they liked. They were very cunning; they would go out and pretend to cut wood and wait until they heard the boys coming, so the boys would cut it for them. Every week on Saturday night there were splendid events, referred to as "Fish Fries." They were the high point of the week: they would be held at someone's house, and everyone would buy fried fish. Afterward there would be a dance.

Lucille attended school in Castlewood in her Junior year, enduring the interminable bus ride over the back roads, doubling back and forth until they picked everyone up and arrived at the county schoolhouse. She almost quit school when Lula Bell's father, her half-brother, would not let them go to the Homecoming Dance. Lucille's "play mother," the principal's wife, had already made her an outfit, and the mother of the boy she was dating gave her a hat and gloves. But her half-brother said it was too far away for girls to go at night. Lucille was so embarrassed over this that she stayed out of school for three weeks. Her classmates wrote letters asking her to come back and the Principal came to see her, saying, "We understand, your brother wouldn't let you go to the Homecoming Dance. But now you'd better get back to school."

Lucille did very well in school; she won second place in a scholarship contest. The Principal and his wife took an interest in her, and they introduced her to one of the professors from Tuskeegee Institute. Had she remained in Castlewood, she would have had a good chance for a scholarship to Tuskeegee. However, she decided not to stay in Castlewood because she could not find any work and besides, she missed her own family.

At home, Lucille sewed and worked as a beautician for the town ladies. She learned to understand "white folk" and to feel comfortable with them. Later, when she became a nurse, she preferred private duty, which involved some freedom of choice and a more personal relationship with a patient, to the routine work and regular hours of staff duty. She never went on to receive her degree as a Registered Nurse (RN); perhaps she absorbed some of her father's attitude toward education.

Lucille has lost touch with Lula Bell; she never returned to Alabama, and Lula Bell moved. But her experiences during her first time away from home left a strong imprint on Lucille's mind, and the memory of that lost opportunity in Castlewood remained, too, reflected in a train ticket to Chicago six or seven years later.

KEEPING UP TIES

Visiting Bus stations, train depots, and more recently, airports in our cities are patronized by large numbers of Black citizens, both affluent and poor, who are usually making journeys related to life, death, social bonding, and work. Since leaving the plantations, and even before, Blacks have been a highly mobile group. In constant search for a niche in a society that is often closed to them, they maintain bonds of kinship and friendship so they may periodically return to renew a feeling of "roots" and so that others may follow them into a new life.

During Lucille's first few months in Chicago she deeply missed her family and the homely atmosphere of Hattiesburg. At first, she went back every six months; then, as the stringent demands of life in Chicago began to take hold, she was able to return only once every year, then every two years. She had a phone installed in her parents' home, for which she paid the monthly bill, so they would keep in touch. She also sent a little money to them each month and to Dora Lee. When they never acknowledged receiving the money, she stopped sending it. She remembered all the ages and birthdates of her family members and sent them cards, but they never reciprocated this act or even thanked her when they received hers. So she thought, "What the heck, they don't care about things like this," and stopped sending those, too. But she still manages to keep in close touch with happenings in Mississippi through her sister, Dora Lee.

Dora Lee lives near her parents. She gets up early every morning before work and has coffee with them. Sometimes their father complains that his wife does not take care of him properly, and he will only accept food or clothing from his daughters. In this way he assures himself of the care and concern of his entire family, which is more important to him than the token exchange of cards and gifts. Dora Lee cooks for him and makes certain that he is taken care of, when he refuses his wife's solicitude; everyone tries to humor him at these times. When he is ill he is convinced that only Lucille can care for him. He will take medicine only if she gives it to him, and only she can persuade him to go to the hospital. So, if her father becomes ill (when he admits it, she knows he really is very ill), she goes home, even if it means losing a job. As she said to another nurse, "I can get another job; I have only one father."

Funerals are occasions on which families get together, particularly in the South. When Lucille's grandmother died, her parents wrote to her and asked her to bring her brothers, Terry and Harlow, down to the funeral. She had a difficult time locating them, since she had lost contact with them. She was angered by their "fooling around" and wasting time. But when they got home, it all seemed worthwhile because their father was rejuvenated. He awoke early the first morning they were there, put on Terry's jeans and went fishing. He refused to wear anything else during their stay, nor would he use his cane. He was delighted to have his family together for the first time in years, and was especially overjoyed to see Terry, who never came home on his own.

When Donna's stepfather died, his funeral in Chicago was large and impressive, but few relatives attended—at least, not "blood" relatives—since few of them were living, but there were many friends and acquaintances, and the Elks conducted an elaborate ceremony. As Lucille remarked, "The Elks were that man's life!" The wake and funeral were held together and, after the service, fried chicken, potato salad, and bourbon were served at the deceased's home. It was a fine funeral, but nothing like those back home. There the wake was not merely a quick glimpse at the body, but a three-day affair, at least, with plenty of food and whiskey. Relatives would come from everywhere and stay for several days or a week.

At her grandmother's funeral, Lucille saw her Aunt Lucille for the first time since she had moved to California. The latter had lived right around the corner from her younger sister, Aretha, while Lucille was growing up, until a second marriage took her to Los Angeles. She returned to Mississippi once before, and they held a reunion, but Lucille could not come because of illness. It seemed to Lucille that every time there was a reunion something happened and she could not attend. When her grandfather died, she was ill and had financial problems. Her family did not notify her of his death or, later, of her father's sister's death, so she would not worry or feel obligated to come to the funerals. She wanted to go to her father's brother's funeral, but again she was financially pressed and could only send flowers. She did get to her grandmother's funeral, which was a highly important family event, and she finally saw Aunt Lucille. She found her to be quite a "swinger," and the two of them sneaked out for a few drinks together and a long talk.

Only once have Lucille's people come to Chicago for a funeral, and that was many years ago when Cousin Wilma, Great-Aunt Sarah's daughter, died in childbirth, and her baby died as well. A few weeks prior to this tragedy, her son died from a rat bite. They held a triple funeral, with baby and mother in one casket. Great-Aunt Sarah lived in Chicago for many years after the tragedy, but has recently sold her house and returned to Mississippi. She liked Chicago, but her family thought it was no place for old people, and certainly no place to die, away from her family.

While Lucille's Southern relatives prefer life in Mississippi, they visit relatives in the North on vacations, as well as for business matters and emergencies. Lucille's mother came to take care of Lucille's youngest son when she was in the hospital for six months. She said she had never seen such a pitiful child as that little boy while his mother was in the hospital: he did not say anything about his mother, but he cried every night. Aretha has traveled to Chicago on several occasions, and Lucille always enjoys her visits. Now that Lucille has grown older, she has come to view her mother from a different perspective. Aretha now treats Lucille as an adult. One thing Lucille really appreciates is that her mother never contradicts her in front of her children. When Lucille's son refused to eat his vegetables, Aretha took Lucille aside quietly and said, "Why force him to eat it if it makes him and you unhappy?"

Almost all of Lucille's relatives on her mother's side have visited in Chicago at one time or another. Aunt Rose came to visit Aunt Louise about thirteen years ago and spent time with Lucille as well. Aretha's oldest brother, Henry, visited once, and her youngest brother, Mervin, has been to Chicago several times. When he was passing through, on his way to Electronics school in Indianapolis, he stopped by for a few days. He looked so old, Lucille did not recognize him, even though he is the same age as she is.

Family Obligations   Uncle Richard, the high school principal, is quite generous. He gave his brother, Mervin, some land in Mississippi for a house. Uncle Richard also partly owns the house Aunt Louise lives in, since he made the downpayment. When Lucille invested her savings in a new house for her parents, Richard reimbursed her for some of the payment she had made on the Contract for Deed. She was surprised and grateful. Uncle Richard had also come to her aid when her niece had refused to go back to Mississippi. Lucille had called him and he had persuaded the girl to leave. Lucille herself rebels a little against Uncle Richard's authority: "I guess he feels he's the boss of the family, but I don't feel he's *my* boss." His mother had always placed a very high value on education, and Richard has achieved highly by her standards.

Uncle Richard is quite a contrast to Uncle John, "the 63d street pimp," as they call him. Even though he never had a job, he always had fine clothes and a car; he was very handsome and well-liked by women. "He's old, now," Lucille relates, "and it's all in his mind, but he'll still make a play for any woman who comes around, even though there's no reason on God's earth why she should want him!"

He was in the army for most of the time that Lucille was growing up. He had many wives at various times and sometimes remarried without having obtained a divorce; he was discharged, probably because of his "messed-up domestic life," Lucille speculates. After his first wife died, he used to send money to his mother. It was a savings to him, since the government matched the amount he sent. But his mother would never give him the money when he came home, so he decided to send it to his sister, Lucille's mother, instead. Then people would come to her for money—brothers, sisters, even Lucille's grandmother—saying that he had agreed to their requests. When he came home on leave, he denied ever having given his consent and berated Aretha for giving away his money. Henceforth, she refused to appropriate any money unless she had written permission from Uncle John. When he came home, she gave him the checks without even having cashed them.

Lucille has one memory about Uncle John that is very pleasant. He once came home on leave with a brand new Pontiac, which he let her drive. Lucille exclaims that she "drove like hell through town, without a license!" He had a great knack for understanding the young. Now he is really not much help to anyone, certainly not to Lucille, although he did come to visit her when she was in the hospital. He stays with Aunt Louise, who is constantly nagging him. He defies her, and does just as he pleases, anyway. "After all," Lucille explains, "that is only his right as a man."

All of these aunts and uncles on her mother's side are influences on Lucille and her siblings whether they live in the North or the South. Her youngest brother, like Uncle Richard, is concerned about getting an education; he has settled down in Hattiesburg after having attended school in Texas. On the other hand, her brother Harlow appears to have some of Uncle John's characteristics. He does not seem to be able to hold down a job, although he appears to be doing all right for himself. Lately, though, he has been "crying the blues"; he has finally left school to join the army, like Uncle John.

Harlow's son, by a common-law wife in Wisconsin, came to Chicago with his mother for a visit, after she and Harlow had separated. Lucille was so taken by Harlow, Jr., who looked just like his father, that she actually tolerated his lazy, temperamental mother for two weeks. The girl managed to alienate everyone, even Dora Lee, who was also visiting at the time. When she left, she took Lucille's good lingerie and left a huge phone bill in return. Lucille was angry, but felt that seeing her nephew was ample compensation for her trouble. She even expressed willingness to take care of him if his mother was not able or did not want to. She knew her brother would not do anything. She had thought that she did not want anything more to do with babies, and often says that she will not be a babysitter when she is a grandmother. But she finds something appealing and reassuring about her own flesh and blood in the form of a little child.

Lucille maintains that her people call her the "mean one" because she is often blunt in expressing her feelings. She has also been labeled a "do-gooder," because she is concerned about everyone in the family. She is "the one they call if anything

The New Place

happens," she claims proudly. She was concerned about her parents' staying another winter in their old house, which was on the verge of collapse. A tornado hit it, nearly causing it to cave in totally, and therefore Lucille renewed her offer of taking up a contract on a new house. Previously, her mother had not heeded this gesture, but now even she was convinced of its necessity. Lucille felt they needed the house more than she did, because her father was ill and at home all day. Thus it was settled, and work began on the new house.

While the house was being built her parents moved in with Dora Lee. Dora Lee's house was crowded, but the old couple refused to stay with Flo, their other daughter, who sometimes has an "attitude" toward her father. Before the end of their stay, however, Aretha surreptitiously went over to Flo's home to take a bath in private—away from Dora Lee's children, who were always omnipresent. Meanwhile, Tang presented himself at the building site every day, watching the progress and "helping out." His wife tried to keep him home; she was afraid that his "help" was more likely a hindrance. But Lucille felt that the builders could handle her father, for they had known him all their lives.

When her parents finally moved into their new house they photographed it and sent the pictures to Lucille. She looked at the photographs doubtfully, but refrained from commenting on them in her letters home, since she did not want to spoil her parents' happiness. When she drove down on Thanksgiving, her fears were realized: the workmanship was shoddy and the materials were cheap. The best that could be said was that it was better than the old house. In any case, her parents were very pleased with it.

Home Town Contacts   Whenever Lucille goes South, she begins by visiting people who live one street down from her mother's house, and then proceeds all around town until she has seen everyone. They all invite her to dinner and she dates often while she is there. Since she is from the city, she carries a certain amount of prestige, just as she did in Castlewood many years ago. The Southern men are nice; they take her to dinner or to a movie or a dance, and then back home. Lucille likes the fact that they do not expect her to jump into bed with them afterward, like they do in Chicago.

Once, in Chicago, she attended an affair given by the Chicago-Hattiesburg Club, a group of people from Hattiesburg who like to get together occasionally. Since the party was in a tavern in her neighborhood, Lucille decided to go. She met an old boyfriend there whom she had dated in the 12th grade (he had been in the 9th grade, but was advanced for his age). He was rather well-to-do and spent his money freely; he had the best wardrobe, dozens of shoes—everything from the best stores. He picked her up on Friday, after work, bringing her a complete outfit—including a hat and gloves—and somehow everything fit her. Then they would go out. Sometimes he fixed dinner for her at his aunt's house, where he lived. He would not let anyone else go near the kitchen and, when he was ready, he sent a taxi for her. When she arrived, her cocktail was ready in the freezer, so the glass would be frosty. "Some of those Hattiesburg men really knew how to treat a woman!" Lucille declared.

Lucille's feelings and recollections about Hattiesburg are tinged with anxiety. She once received a phone call from a friend she grew up with, who is an Evan-

Grand Kids

gelist. She periodically asks Lucille whether she has been "saved" and is "ready to meet her maker"; characteristically, Lucille replies with a terse "no." On this occasion the woman said she felt something was wrong with Lucille's people in Mississippi. She asked for their phone number, and Lucille gave it to her just in case something really were wrong. She did not call herself, though, because that would indicate that she was superstitious and besides, she felt sure Dora Lee would have contacted her if something had happened. At the time she was concerned about her youngest sister, Flo, who was pregnant and had a kidney infection; her mother, who was suffering from a heart condition, diabetes, high blood pressure, and cancer; and her father, who was merely old. But she did not want to allow herself to be governed by her fears.

Whenever Lucille hears Willie Banks, the "too late" man from Jackson, Mississippi, and his Southernaires, she thinks about her family, and especially about her brother, Terry. She goes to hear him every year at the Baptist Church; she cries when he sings about the man who waits too long to go home. When he finally does, it is too late: his mother is dead.

Death of a Matriarch   When Lucille's grandmother was stricken with her last and fatal illness, her son, Mervin, phoned Aunt Louise in Chicago even before he informed his sisters in Mississippi. Louise left for Hattiesburg right away, without notifying Lucille. When Lucille heard that Aunt Louise was in Mississippi, she knew there must be something seriously wrong, because Aunt Louise had already been down once that year. Lucille had not as yet answered Dora Lee's last letter and still had not called home. She was filled with uneasiness and uncertainty, unlike her usually decisive self. Then Earline called, for she had spoken to Aretha and had learned that Lucille's grandmother was ill. Ordinarily, Earline's intrusion into family matters would have irritated Lucille but, in this case, she almost welcomed it, because she had been secretly worried about her father.

When Aretha phoned from Hattiesburg with the news of her mother's death, Lucille felt relieved at having definite knowledge and being able to make plans. About five carloads of people were going down to the funeral, she discovered; she hesitated about driving, since she did not think her brothers would help pay for gas. She finally contacted Terry, who said he would let her know whether he was going the next day; he did not call back. When at last she reached Harlow in Wisconsin, he said he would "hock some things" and fly to Chicago. Meanwhile, she worried that she would miss her ride with Cousin Tom, while waiting for those two. Then, suddenly, Terry appeared, and Lucille decided to drive after all. Gradually, the family forces gathered for the long trek to Mississippi.

After their grandmother's death, Dora Lee lapsed into a state of depression. Lucille was disturbed about her: she felt that Dora Lee drank too much and did not assert herself enough. She was usually quiet and easy-going. However, sometimes after she had too much to drink, Dora Lee came home and forced her husband to leave the house.

Lucille feels that all families should be close-knit. She is very proud of the pictures of her mother, father, sisters, and brothers, which were taken at the time of her grandmother's funeral: they are a fine-looking family! Even Terry briefly came out of exile to get copies of the picture. But basically, Lucille laments, since she came to Chicago she feels like an orphan.

REFLECTIONS ON "LIFELINE"

Some principles can be elicited from the description of Lucille's family which are also found in other families in the study, although they are not, in some instances, so clearly manifest. Lucille's membership in an extended kin group, particularly on her mother's side, is shown by her deep involvement in the events taking place in Mississippi; her financial commitment, as well as that of her maternal uncle, indicates that family obligations of a significant order extend beyond the nuclear household.

Social anthropologists may see in Lucille's family traces of matrilineal kinship organization, based on joint land ownership and economic cooperation within a group of brothers and sisters, in which children belong to their mother's kin group and a maternal uncle has jural authority over, and takes responsibility for, his sisters' children. This seems to hold true for Lucille's mother's side and, perhaps to a lesser extent, for her father's family. The affectionate character of Lucille's relationship with her father and her father's mother while she was growing up, contrasted with the more authoritarian overtones of her relations with her mother, her mother's mother, and her mother's brother all suggest a matrilateral orientation. The act of sending Lucille to stay with her paternal relatives, possibly because of growing sibling rivalry or merely because she was "difficult," is reminiscent of a similar, though reversed, practice in the patrilateral Pakistani family—sending a first son to stay with his mother's kin group at the birth of a second son. The death of the old grandmother—the focus of the extended family—brings together the entire kin group. As in the case of funerals generally, showing respect for the dead is, at the same time, the occasion for renewal of bonds among the living.

The tension that often exists between affinal kin is suggested by the "pollution" concept (expressed by Lucille and her mother) surrounding the food cooked by Lucille's father's sister. Brother Terry's lack of stability and goal commitments underscores the plight of an individual alienated from his family in a society with solidarity of kin groups. His situation is particularly poignant to Lucille because of his potential for playing a powerful role in her family as her eldest brother. Perhaps it is precisely the pressures of that role, given the family personalities, which have resulted in his alienation.

In other families, a patrilateral emphasis is apparent (see Chapter 3, Dean and Lois; Chapter 5, Charles' family; and Chapter 6, Sally's in-laws), while in some a truly bilateral organization is present (see Chapter 6, Lois McCoy). Although it is tempting to see continuations of African patrilineal, matrilineal, and bilineal traditions, resulting in an "ambilineal" system, it should be stressed that the American Black family was fashioned in the crucible of slavery; whatever its antecedents were, they were not as compelling as conditions in the New World. Still, people build on what they know, and possibly here and there a custom, a rule, or a value survived as a foundation for a new way of life.

2 / Men and women

INTRODUCTION

The nature of the love relationship between a man and a woman reveals much about the character of a society. Since it develops relatively late in life, it is conditioned by other important relationships, and furthermore, it reveals the attitude of a people toward the future and the means by which they prepare for social continuity. The Black male-female relationship can be seen here as a dialectic, in which both positions must be firmly defined and articulated before a resolution—which, in turn, is open to change—can be attained. Thus, family and society are given structure through a strong male-female role identity which is, however, not static, but continuously being redefined.

When kinship relationships are strong, perhaps there is more scope for the free expression of feelings and passion in a love relationship; in a sense, there is not as much at stake. Certainly, Black Americans have glorified romantic and erotic love to its highest expression, and have utilized the binding and healing qualities of sex to great advantage. But underlying the emotive expression is a fundamental honesty and a desire to work out a satisfactory compact between lovers, rather than to accept an imposed one. There is a concern for individual freedom and self-awareness, a determination not to be "turned around" that is highly comprehensible, given the history of Black Americans.

"BE MY BABY"

Romantic Love: Pleasures and Vicissitudes "Soul music" radio stations are an inspired voice of Black people in Chicago. In the summer, their sounds ring out from passing cars, from the open windows of stifling flats, and from transistor radios carried by young "soul" brothers and sisters sauntering along the street. The young seem to know the songs instinctively, and often burst into spirited, precise renditions in the middle of a phrase; the adults show recognition, approval, or amusement. What is the message of these songs with such universal appeal? They are about life, especially about the love of man for woman and woman for man. The young learn them quickly by imitation; the older people reminisce and enjoy them.

29

"I can sing a rainbow," sings a vibrating male voice as he paints the spectrum of love's emotions. "The thrill is gone . . ." laments a favorite blues singer. "I heard it through the grapevine . . ." accuses a lover: she might at least have told him herself that she had fallen in love with another. "That's the way love is," it seems, and "Everybody plays the fool" at sometime in his life. But a wise voice warns: Beware of the one who informs on your love—what is his motive? The best response is "Run yo' shoes over (and let me run my business)."

Despite its vicissitudes, love endures: "Chains of love," sings the perennial lover; and a long-suffering mate asks, "What's the use of breaking up?" Lady Soul sets the terms: A "Do-right, all-day woman" deserves a "Do-right, all-night man." She pledges that they will always be bound together and captures the poignancy of a parting, entreating him to call her the moment he arrives. Reassurance comes from the bright, young ones, "Someday we'll be together" and "I'll be there."[1]

The message of these direct, many-faceted lyrics is that man needs woman, woman needs man, and that despite heart-ache and betrayal, they are indivisible. Only the Black singer can convey the depth and breadth of the love of a Black man for his woman; only the Black songstress can truly portray the dilemmas and needs of the Black woman in dealing with her man.

Love between a man and a woman can be divided into three stages: first is the time of romance, when the relationship is challenging and exciting and the lovers are transformed into wonderful new beings! Then comes the testing—the demands, proposals, and compromises; by the end of this stage, which may last months or years, the decision is made as to whether the relationship, with mutual accommodations, should be continued into a third stage of relative stability, or dissolved. For Black lovers the second stage is often more searching and extended than for their White counterparts, since roles are defined less by convention and more by individual needs. The initial romance and excitement is often sufficiently intense to ensure an attachment that may blossom into a lasting relationship, overcoming odds which may seem overwhelming.

When Sylvester Charles met Lucille Foster he needed a woman; that is, he needed the security and satisfaction that comes from loving one woman, as well as the extension of his own experience by sharing life with another. He appeared to be in a desirable position, having a great deal of freedom and few domestic responsibilities. Since he had separated from his wife, he had been living with his parents; his mother took care of his two sons and his wife had charge of their daughter. He was no longer satisfied with casual affairs, he was ready for a deep relationship with a woman.

Lucille had been separated from her husband for many years. Her son, Robert, was in his early teens; she also had a son from a love affair that ended abruptly

---

[1] Following are the songs which are mentioned above and the singers who made them hits at the time of this study: "I Can Sing a Rainbow," The Dells; "The Thrill Is Gone," B. B. King; "I Heard It through the Grapevine," Marvin Gaye; "That's the Way Love Is," Marvin Gaye; "Everybody Plays the Fool," The Main Ingredient; "Run Yo Shoes Over (And Let Me Run My Business)," Joe Tex; "Chains of Love," Bobby Bland; "What's the Use of Breaking Up," Little Milton; "Do-Right Woman, Do-Right Man," Aretha Franklin; "You and Me," Aretha Franklin; "Call Me" Aretha Franklin; "Someday We'll Be Together," Diana Ross and the Supremes; "I'll Be There," The Jackson Five.

with his birth, five years previously. On the day of Arnold's birth, she discovered that his father was married and living with his wife. The fact that he was married came as no surprise to her; technically, so was she. But when she learned that he was actually living with his wife she felt that he had "put her in the 'trick bag.'" She had visited him at his friends' apartment, where he was supposed to be staying, and had even cooked for him there. They had not made love there, but she still felt that he had humiliated her in the eyes of those people, and she never forgave Lewison. After that experience, she was hesitant about forming attachments with men.

She met Sylvester Charles when he was a patient in the hospital where she worked as a nurse. They were attracted to each other: he by her vibrant personality and capable manner, and she by his hazel eyes and shy smile. After he recovered from his illness, they continued seeing each other. Lucille had experienced only one brief, unsatisfying affair since she had broken up with Lewison, and she had not been seeing any man for more than a year. Despite her bad luck with men, she was vulnerable and wanted a man's love. Arnold had reached an age where he no longer needed as much of her attention and she needed a man to care for. She fell deeply in love with Sylvester.

The first two years of their relationship were idyllic. Lucille was so much in love that, when Sylvester came to pick her up at work, "her face would start sweating and her hair stood on end," so that she would have to comb it. To Sylvester, Lucille was everything he admired and coveted: she was educated, she displayed an easy manner with people of all stations, and she expressed herself openly and freely. He could not offer her status or great wealth, but he could give her glorious moments of happiness. Their lovemaking was ecstatic, and the places in which they celebrated their love took on special qualities of romance. They were able to carry on the less glamorous tasks of their routine lives with some amount of grace.

Black men and women often love intensely; and these favored or "cursed" ones as the mood may be, do not give up easily on love. They continue to pursue an elusive dream of happiness throughout a lifetime of unfulfilled beginnings, sometimes to a happy ending. But in any event, they can look back on a grand adventure of the spirit, which may play havoc with the stability of the conjugal tie, but which often contributes to the balance and wisdom of the person.

A Black woman once commented with surprise upon the loveless life of an attractive White spinster: "A Black woman always has a man; she may be old and have only one eye or leg, but she'll always have a man somehow." An exaggeration, perhaps, but if a Black woman is without a man it probably will not be a permanent condition, given the propensities of the man, her own needs, and their willingness to face the truth about themselves!

A Lifetime Quest: Harriet Lucille's friend, Harriet, had three children by three different men, but she never really found a mate among the fathers of her children. She married while young and pregnant, for the sake of respectability, but the marriage was short-lived. She and her husband had lived with her parents after they married, and her father, who worked with her husband, used to talk about the women his son-in-law was seeing. Later, when they moved out on their own, her husband would not give her much money for food and at times he would not pay the rent. She therefore started to work, and they went their own ways, with little communication. Harriet felt that he did not take any interest in his family; he never kept his promises to them, either before or after the separation. His daughter, however, has kept in touch with him and she still receives money from him occasionally.

Harriet was ignorant about men when she was married. Her father had instilled her with a fear of boys while she was growing up, telling her they might kidnap her or hurt her in some way—anything to keep her from getting involved with boys. When she was married, she had no idea of what to expect from a man but, whatever it was, it could not be good. She did not know how to deal with her husband in the day-to-day crises that arose, nor was he able to help.

After her divorce, Harriet dated an older, married man, whose wife was in Huntsville, Alabama. She met him at a hotel where they were both employed. Jackson had come up North to be with his father, who was dying of tuberculosis in a sanitarium. The old man lived longer than expected and, after he died, Jackson decided to stay on, because he could not make as much money at home. In some ways he was like a father to Harriet; he gave her security and affection, and taught her not to be afraid of men.

Harriet's relationship with Jackson lasted eight years. During this time, she had become somewhat bored and began to see other men. She describes her affair with the father of her son as merely "hit and run"; she never really attempted to contact him afterward. She was in love with Alex, the father of her youngest daughter, Carla. He was light-skinned, with light brown eyes, and very handsome. Harriet, who was dark-skinned, felt herself unattractive, although she kept herself well-groomed and dressed attractively. In her relationship with Alex, Harriet was the one to give affection; her partner was cold and inflexible. When Carla was born, he refused to accept her as his child. Harriet filed a paternity suit against him, which she lost, because the lie detector test that she took showed that Harriet had been seeing Jackson. The judge asked to see Jackson, but he refused, saying he did not want to "stick his neck out." If the judge had seen him, he would have known that Carla was not his child; she had light skin and eyes like her father. But understandably, Jackson did not want to help Harriet in her attempt to put a claim on another man. And that ended their eight-year relationship—she never saw him again.

Alex did not come to see Harriet until the child was two or three years old. Then he started coming over often and acting "crazy" like he wanted to start an affair all over again. Now he was the one to show affection; Harriet was cold. She had lost all feeling for him and only asked for money now and then for tuition at Carla's nursery school.

By this time, Harriet was seeing several men, all of whom gave her money or helped her out in various ways. These were strictly "business arrangements," which helped her and her children along and which helped tide her through the lonely, manless years. Among these men was her insurance agent, whom she liked, and who paid her premiums, and an older White businessman, who was married; she saw him "off and on" throughout the years, but only on Saturdays and Sundays. She felt that White men were more respectful of women than were Black men. She reasoned that Black men probably resented the fact that women often held down the jobs men should have had. They seemed to have more respect for White women, with whom they were not in competition. She felt that Black men, especially younger ones, were too bold and outspoken; they did not seem to care about anything and were quick to take advantage of you.

Harriet had several other men friends whom she saw occasionally; she liked some of them, others not particularly. She had few inhibitions about sex; her cooly professional view of these "arrangements" sharply contrasts with Lucille's scruples. She did insist on cleanliness, however, and forced the untidier men to bathe. Afterwards, if they wanted to give her money, she would take it and send them on their way.

Despite her distrust of men, these relationships were empty for Harriet; she needed love. Both Jackson and Alex had been considerably older than Harriet and she felt the need for a change. This time she chose a man ten years younger than she was. He lived in her housing project, and they met on the stairway one New Year's Eve day, when she was on her way to work. He was taking his mother to the South Side and offered to give her a lift. She invited him to her sister's house for "chitlins" after she finished work. He accepted, and they "courted" for over two years.

Harriet always looked forward to their lovemaking: she was deeply in love. But he started bringing girls to his apartment, even while she was at home and then began to see another woman in the Project, across the way. She told him, "I don't expect you to be an angel, but at least you could be with me when I'm home." Of course, she continued seeing other men, discreetly, but they did not mean anything to her. She thought that perhaps his mother had said something to him about the other men. Anyway, she decided that she could not endure his insults any longer and broke up with him.

Breaking up was painful: none of Harriet's male friends could soothe her feelings. She was aware of his being at the other woman's place every night. He did not have any respect for women, she felt. Apparently, he expected to move in with every woman with whom he had an affair. She would not let a man stay at her house like that. When she saw his mother wearing the raincoat she had bought for him, she felt deeply hurt. Later, feeling a need to vent her frustrations, she reported him for never having filed his income tax!

After that affair, Harriet really felt bitter about men. She discussed the topic of men's failings with Lucille, who was having problems with Sylvester, and together they decided that men were not worth the trouble. Harriet felt that she was too old to think in terms of anything but sexual satisfaction, but she found few men who were even suitable for that. Only younger men could really satisfy, she felt, and she did not have much to offer them, either financially or emotionally, because the young need love desperately, even though they may seem to reject it. The demands and risks with young men were too great for what they gave in return.

Mutual Needs After about a year, Harriet moved and her life changed dramatically. She had placed her name on a waiting list for an apartment in a new

The Project

middle-income project that was being built nearby, and her turn finally came. Her salary as an attendant in a convalescent home was not sufficient to pay the bills, however, and Harriet found she had to deal with considerably higher rent, moving expenses, and new furniture.

Harriet loved her new apartment and set about decorating it with a passion that had been long frustrated. She finally had what she wanted—a beautiful place for herself and her children. But the bills mounted up and pressures from her creditors grew. For the first time since her marriage, she thought in terms of setting up residence with a man. She needed a mature, settled man who would be willing to help her out.

About this time Harriet met an old school friend who had broken up with his wife. Both he and Harriet had been "turned around" many times and both knew what they wanted. They treated each other with restraint and respect, and Harriet began the difficult task of compromising her independence and domestic authority for the sake of a new and desired life style. She did not expect love and faithful-

Middle-Income Housing

ness, just financial and moral support. She sometimes resented and rebelled against a man's needs and prerogatives in her household; still, deep inside, she felt a pleasure that went beyond her joy in her physical environment. For a time, at least, despite her doubts and complaints, she rather enjoyed taking care of a man and being the subject of a man's concern.

NEGOTIATIONS

Domestic Problems and Compromises: Lucille and Sylvester A Black woman often faces a dilemma in dealing with her man: she wants him to be strong, to protect and support her, but not to control her; yet, because of his economic situation, control over a woman may sometimes be crucial to a Black man's survival. Further, being supported temporarily by a woman is not necessarily detrimental to a Black man's image, nor is his periodic inability or unwillingness to support a woman until he has made what he feels to be a definite commitment. He may continue to maintain his independence indefinitely, regarding the role of provider as an important alternative but a luxury he cannot afford; even when he sees it as a positive option he is wary of being caught in a domestic trap. Therefore, he may give money to more than one woman at a time, "spreading around" his largess, so to speak, over more than one household.

The Black woman, fully aware of these conditions, strives to attain the optimum situation for herself and her man. To do this, she must often work harder than her White counterpart: she must be cognizant of all the pertinent facts in her environment; she must be adroit in logic and rhetoric and adept in recognizing and taking advantage of opportunities whenever they arise. Contrary to the beliefs of some, in relation to her man, the Black woman is strong but not dominant; he maintains his spiritual autonomy, thus his manhood.

Because of the circumstances of their existence, marriage may come hard to Black men and women. A first marriage may be early but brief, leaving in its wake unresolved feelings and problems that must be worked out later. The decision by a man and woman to develop a relationship is necessarily complex and is marked by a range of external arrangements, depending upon the seriousness of the intent and the stage of the relationship.

When a man moves into a woman's household, it may signify a number of things. In any case, it must be an economic benefit to either or both of them. Generally, since the woman must make the greatest accommodation, she should benefit from the arrangement. However, if her emotional needs outweigh her financial needs, she may take a man in for little return. If she has her eye on a possible permanent arrangement and marriage, she may be moderate in her demands, even though her later attempts to increase them may meet with failure. There are many types of arrangements, both physical and financial, and often the situation is fluid.

Sylvester Charles began to stay overnight at Lucille's apartment one night when there was a big snowstorm. She told him he could sleep on the sofa. After that, he stayed over every night. Lucille had ambivalent feelings about letting a man to whom she was not married stay with her. She was afraid that the children might awaken and hear something. When her mother came to visit, she wanted to ask Sylvester to stay with his mother, but Aretha said, "Whether or not I approve, if this is Sylvester's home he must stay here." So he remained, but he slept on the sofa.

When Sylvester moved in—"moved his clothes in"—as Lucille referred to it, he actually left most of his possessions at his mother's house, where he stopped by after work to get what he needed for the next few days. This arrangement continued, with some variation, throughout their relationship. When Lucille noticed one of his dress suits in the closet, she speculated as to Sylvester's plans: was he going to take her out or was he going to a party? Sometimes she washed his clothes and sometimes his mother washed them; occasionally, he took them to the laundry. Lucille's domestic contributions were, in a sense, a favor rather than an obligation, because, after all, they were not married.

Sylvester ate dinner at Lucille's house; she was a good cook. After he took a second job, she began to fix his lunch from the dinner leftovers. When she felt especially loving, or after they had quarreled and made up, she might fry a chicken or cook a ham and take the hot food to him at night. She did not do that very often, since she had to be at work at 7 A.M. every day.

Sylvester gave Lucille money for food and paid some of the utility bills. He did not always give the same amount of money, nor did he give it consistently. At times Lucille asked him for it: she should not take his contribution for granted, just as he should not take her favors lightly. In this way they were giving of themselves and not merely living up to someone's expectations of what they should do. If Sylvester did not give her money for groceries, Lucille would just buy a few things for herself and the children. Eventually, he came through. Sometimes, when they had been having problems, he did the grocery shopping on his day off, especially if it was on a Saturday, when Lucille had to work. He paid too much for everything, Lucille felt, and wasted money on nonessentials. Still, she appreciated his help.

When Lucille complained that he did not give her enough money or that he did not stay home enough, Sylvester did not alter his behavior to conform to her wishes. That was not a part of the bargain. Instead, he chose some other way to show that he appreciated her, such as taking her out or showing affection, since he was usually rather undemonstrative. Even when she was angry with him, Lucille was careful to see that his dinner was prepared and that there was enough left over for his lunch. This, like Sylvester's financial help, was a part of their agreement.

Whenever the two of them discussed marriage, Lucille made clear the conditions under which she would consider it, which involved much more financial support and interest in the home on his part. Later on, when she and Sylvester were having troubles, Lucille fastened on the details of their unwritten and, in part, unspoken agreement like a lawyer, to show that he had been the one to break faith.

For two years things had gone well with them, until Sylvester took a night job. Then their problems began. She was alone in the evenings. She thought that, when he went out at night, he could always *say* he was going to work, when in reality he might be out drinking with his buddies and seeing some of the women at the project. He was supposed to finish work at 1 A.M., but sometimes he did not get home until 4 or even 6 in the morning. He never called to let her know that he was going to be late. One night he said he had to wait for the juvenile authorities, because he had been having troubles with some of the teenagers. Lucille wondered how he and his friends could possibly protect people and gain the respect of younger men, when all they did, was drink and carouse around. If those youngsters respected him, they would not break his car windows like they did. She complained, "They're nothing but a bunch of drunks and whores down there. To think, they're supposed to represent the law to the younger men and tell them what to do and what not to do."

Sylvester had more money after he took his second job. He bought a new car and a tape deck, but he did not give Lucille any more money. She became angry when she was broke and she knew he had a "pocketful of money." She suspected that he was spending it on other women.

Lucille and Sylvester helped each other in other than domestic matters. When they first met, Lucille did not own a car and Sylvester let her drive his part of the time. Later, when she got her own car, she returned the favor while his was being repaired, even when it meant a certain amount of inconvenience and curtailment of her activities. She also helped him out in his personal business matters, because she had more education than he did. Once, after they had broken up, he "got back in" by asking her to write to his insurance company about his broken car window. She told him she would always help him out in any way she could, even if they were not going together. She felt that when she needed him he was not always there. She decided that her next man was going to think she was totally helpless, and incapable of doing a thing!

No one who saw Lucille laying linoleum rugs in her kitchen, bedroom, and living room, with the help of her two sons whom she closely supervised, would have believed that she was helpless. She seemed to enjoy a display of self-sufficiency, which was also an act of self-protection. Sylvester or no Sylvester, she seemed to be saying, Lucille was still boss in her own home.

Family Involvement and Interference Lucille became acquainted with Sylvester's family soon after they started going together. She especially liked Mr. Charles, his father, whom she gave a Father's Day gift every year. She also got along fairly well with his mother. She did not like his sister, Janet, who was always calling and asking for Sylvester. Lucille and Janet used to be "tight," until the latter started "running around on her husband," whom she told that she had been with Lucille, when in fact Lucille had not seen her for three weeks. That cooled Lucille off. Further, Janet was constantly making demands on Sylvester, asking him to take her somewhere or to lend her his car. Janet called Lucille to ask whether she was going with Sylvester on his vacation. When Lucille said that she was not going, Janet replied that she and her parents would probably go with him. Lucille was incensed. An aunt of Sylvester's warned him that Lucille would always make him feel inferior because she was more educated than he. Lucille never liked that aunt and tried to avoid being home whenever she and her husband came to call. She certainly did not help Sylvester's self-image at all, Lucille felt.

Sylvester and Lucille used to take vacations together; they traveled to Mississippi to see her family or to St. Louis to see his relatives. Lucille's family liked Sylvester; her father was always at his side. He teased Sylvester about being henpecked because he always asked Lucille's permission before he went anywhere. Lucille remarked that he never did that in Chicago.

After a while, Lucille and Sylvester began to take separate vacations. Because Lucille had gone to Nassau, where she had a marvelous time and met many attractive men, she was more willing to let Sylvester go on his vacation without her. She could not afford to take the time off from work, and he did not offer to help her out with paying the bills if she did want to go. First he took his family back East to visit his sister. When he returned he asked Lucille to accompany him to St. Louis. She refused, saying that she wanted to go to Detroit to visit her relatives instead. Sylvester went without her, leaving suddenly one day without warning.

Diplomacy and Other Means   Lucille was a seasoned diplomat. Whenever she refused one of Sylvester's offers, she would explain why it was not acceptable and would make a counteroffer. Even when Sylvester would not budge from his position, he was left with the vague feeling that he was in the wrong, and that he would have to make amends at some later date. In this way, Lucille tried to maintain her ground, although often Sylvester merely ran from the situation, leaving her an empty field of combat.

While Sylvester was in St. Louis, Lou, a friend of his, called Lucille and told her many things about him, some of which she believed, some of which she did not. He said that Sylvester was seeing a twenty-year-old girl who was on his bowling team and that he had let her kiss him in public when he made a strike. He reported that Sylvester had taken another woman with him to St. Louis and that Sylvester had said that Lucille had demanded money in order to go with him. That was a lie, Lucille asserted: she had not asked him for anything. She was not even sure that he paid the electric bill, which was his responsibility!

Lou described a credit game that Sylvester was engaged in at work—lending money to people until payday and charging them interest. Apparently, Lou did not care much for these activities: the moneylender is never popular. Sylvester was breaking a code of friendship and, worse, was fairly successful at it. Lucille did not approve either; she was especially disappointed to learn that Sylvester had made a lot of money last month, and yet had not offered to give her anything extra to take care of things at home, so that she could go along with him.

Lucille decided she had had enough of Sylvester's dealings. She packed up his clothes, wrote him a letter, and took them to his mother's house. This was not the first time she had done this. A friend of hers joked about how mean she was to Sylvester: "I don't know why you pack his bags and put them outside the door when you mean to take him back. Poor Sylvester comes back with his tail between his legs." (She imitated a man acting as though he were surrounded by overwhelming, implacable forces.) The previous time Lucille had put him out, she had won a bet with friends about how long the separation would last. She had occasionally threatened Sylvester. For instance, one evening Sylvester wanted Lucille to go out with him, but she refused because she had to go to work the next day. He said, "Well, I'm going," and started to get dressed. Lucille did not like this idea, and she said, "Get *all* your things: I'm going to put them in the middle of the floor and you can take them with you if you go out that door!" He started to slow up then and she went up to him and started to take off his tie and to unbutton his coat. He held up his arms so she could unbutton his sleeve and said, "You might as well take off my pants too." She replied, "You'll have to take off your shoes; I won't do that." She felt that he was really glad that he did not have to go out.

At times when Lucille was angry, she would comment, "If all I wanted was sex I could go out and get it on any streetcorner." But at other times she would admit that Sylvester "really could do it" and left little doubt that she, too, was accomplished in the art of lovemaking, although she was seldom explicit about details.

Whenever Lucille moved him out, Sylvester was careful to let her know he was staying with his mother; he wanted to be sure of getting back in. He came back gradually—calling, dropping by, "sneaking" a few clothes in, then settled back into a routine, treading lightly for a while. Once, when they were making up, he was about to take her to a motel when she decided that she wanted to go home. He deliberately misinterpreted her, she insisted, thinking she wanted him to go home with her. He stayed there that night and continued staying again after that.

Apparently, Sylvester was fairly satisfied with things as they were. Although Lucille was willing to let him come back time after time, she was unhappy. She started seeing other men. They were married and not attractive to her in a romantic sense, but, since she was still in love with Sylvester it did not matter. They were generous with her—she saw to that—taking her out on the lonely nights and giving her presents and a little cash, but they had to satisfy her sexually, as well. Lucille was an active partner, implying with vigorous gestures that her feats in bed resembled, at times, those of an acrobat! But in some ways she was quite conservative about the sexual act: she expressed disgust when she learned that one of her male friends "ate trim" (oral sex). After her discovery, she maintained a strictly platonic relationship with him, and she ridiculed him unmercifully when talking to her women friends.

The Meaning of Marriage Lucille grew more and more dissatisfied with her arrangement with Sylvester. She thought, "I've got a boyfriend and a man on the side: Where is it getting me? I don't have any security, and the little amount of money these men are giving me makes me like a whore."

Lucille decided to get a divorce and straighten out her life. She spoke to the priest about this, saying, "I want a divorce: I can't go on living like this. I don't care whether I'll be married in the eyes of the church or not. I can't take communion, anyway, because I'm committing adultery. I can't ask forgiveness for something when I'm going to do it, anyway." Lucille was a relatively recent convert to Catholicism, and she could not always accept the views of the church on matters of sex and marriage. The priest answered her: "We don't *know* what we're going to do; we can only try not to do it," thus giving her an out. But Lucille was too honest about matters of sex; she knew she would not even try. She was 36 years old and, as she put it, "Nobody 36 years old is going to give up screwing unless there's something wrong with them."

Marriage had been a matter of much discussion and concern throughout Lucille's relationship with Sylvester, although neither had obtained a divorce. They each had to define what marriage meant to them and their definitions had to be acceptable to each other before they took such a step. At one time they had decided to marry and Sylvester had informed Lucille's sons about their plans. The youngest, Arnold, had been thrilled; he liked Sylvester and was pleased with the idea of having a father. But the oldest son, Robert, displayed an "attitude." He said that he was not marrying her and therefore it was none of his affair. When Sylvester told Lucille about Robert's response, they decided against marriage, feeling that it probably would not work out as long as Robert was at home, since he plainly did not like Sylvester.

After that attempt, things had deteriorated. Lucille decided to broach the subject of marriage again one day and went into the bathroom while Sylvester was shaving, told him abruptly that she wanted to get married, and then walked out. He called after her, "so you've changed your mind," and went to telephone his lawyer, presumably to start making arrangements for a divorce. Lucille also went ahead with her plans for a divorce; she was not sure that she and Sylvester would ever marry, she admitted, since he was not "ready." But she was tired of living like she was and thought that if it was not him, it would be someone else.

She wanted to buy a house; she had seen a townhouse that required a very low downpayment. She and Sylvester were supposed to go to look at one together, but he never mentioned it and she did not want to pressure him. She had regarded it as a first step toward matrimony, but evidently Sylvester had not. He asked her if she would like to "go in with him" on a townhouse and she got very angry. Lucille became indignant, "Imagine his asking a single girl if she'd go in with him on a house as a partner: what did that sound like?"

Sylvester apologized for his blunder. Sometimes the niceties of convention eluded him; besides, Lucille was inconsistent at times, interpreting the proprieties to suit herself. He had just moved back into her apartment and was somewhat cautious. They discussed marriage and she asked him if he was afraid of it. He admitted he had been because of "the changes she could go through," but he now decided that he could handle it. Lucille wondered aloud if he thought he could continue as he was if they married and he replied that he knew he would have .to try harder. She said that things would have to change *drastically* if they married. She would not want to work all the time, but just enough to help out. Then Sylvester said he wanted to have his two sons with him, but Lucille balked at that idea. She could not see herself sitting home with four children while he ran around.

Still, Lucille was on "cloud nine" after their talk; she felt that perhaps they might make it, after all. For the first time in ages she and Sylvester sat down and had dinner together. She almost started to sharpen the knife to carve the ham, but asked Sylvester to do it instead. She remarked several times about how happy she was that he was there for dinner. Arnold was at the table and he glowed with happiness; he whispered to his mother that Sylvester, who remained expressionless and said nothing, probably had not heard her remarks. Robert was not at the table.

Breakdown of Negotiations This happy state of affairs did not continue for very long. When Sylvester failed to come home until six o'clock one morning, Lucille told him he did not have to come at all. The worst thing a man could do to her was to stay out all night. She told him she knew he was seeing another woman and, further, she knew where the girl lived. Some acquaintances who lived in the girl's neighborhood said she had been talking about Sylvester rather indiscreetly. Lucille could have exposed them that night, she claimed, but she did not want to do so in public. He replied that he did not believe her: if he had been in her place he would not have hesitated to confront them. She explained, "You're a man and you could make it very embarrassing for me. I have children and I wouldn't want them to think their mother was going to jail over a man." She had her domestic responsibilities to think about. Sylvester said he understood her situation, but he continued to deny her accusations.

Sylvester had been really angry about the earlier "leak" concerning his activities, and threatened to "get out his gun" if he found out who it was that called her. He asked Lucille to accompany him bowling and made sure that the alleged twenty-year-old was nowhere around. Up to now, Lucille had always said that she only suspected that he was "fooling around," but could not prove it. Now, she asserted, she knew it for sure. She was still very careful about the men she was seeing. She never let them come to the house and they could only call at certain times. The drama of their love life played itself out, on a "downward trend," but even in its ebb, it occasionally brought reflections of earlier happiness.

When Lucille finally got her divorce she tried to persuade Sylvester to leave. At first, she did not force him out. He could not seem to make up his mind about marriage. She told him, "There isn't much sex going on around here, so you must be getting it on the outside." He said, "That could go for you, too," and she replied, "That's just why I brought it up." He finally admitted to seeing someone, and when she pushed him, he further admitted that it could develop into something. Before he had always said that no other woman could ever mean anything to him.

Things kept dragging on, with both of them seeing others on the side, until finally Lucille decided to put a stop to it and asked him to leave for the last time. Afterward, Sylvester kept calling Lucille and telling her that he could not live without her. He nearly proved his claim by getting involved in a serious auto accident. Lucille let him use her car, then, but refused to let him come back. She was seeing a married man at the time, who she informed that she would continue to see Sylvester, because he was single and had more to offer in a future. But obviously, Sylvester was not ready to marry.

Neither Lucille nor Sylvester had surrendered their autonomy; both had stopped short of total commitment. They each had maintained "face" and they could now turn elsewhere with a minimum of self-reproach and recriminations. Lucille met an unmarried man whom she liked; she guessed that he was living with a woman, but she did not care about that—she was never again going to let a man stay in her apartment unless they were married. She had not solved the problem of marriage, but at least she was free to accept such an alternative if it came her way.

If one is negotiating, it must be from a position of strength. A young woman who was married presented this view:

> I think a woman should have some independence; maybe a man will think twice about leaving her if he knows she can get along without him. She should work to get things for her family they couldn't get otherwise; then she'll know things, too, and can help her children out; she'll know what to tell them later in life when they have problems. She should always have a savings account her husband doesn't know about, put in a little bit here, a little bit there, so she can buy herself something, a dress or something. And if a bill is due and

her husband says, "Go tell them I'll get it to them Tuesday," she can go ahead and pay it and then take the money he gives her Tuesday. And if he leaves she'll have something to tide her over. Every woman should have her own savings account.

A boyfriend of her sister's who overheard this statement, took exception to it. "If it's a mutual thing, they can't be hiding things like that. The time is bound to come when he'll ask her, 'Where did you get the money for this?' and she'll have to tell him." The young woman disagreed: "No, if she works it right, he'll never have to know. He can do the same thing if he wants; I know I can do it and tell a story that would make you believe me, too." The young man was not convinced, saying "It just won't work."

The young lady was having problems with her husband. She was trying to finish high school and to train herself for some kind of work, since she could not support her child. She keenly felt the helplessness of her situation: her husband, who was supporting the child, tried to keep her from seeing him. She was learning at a tender age the same lesson that Lucille and Harriet had learned so well: never again would she be so completely dependent on a man when she had no bargaining power.

TOGETHER AND APART

The Perennial Nature of Love The lyrics of a popular song lament that win or lose, love is an illusion: the lover really does not know love at all. This is a familiar, but in my view, not a Black complaint and does not express a Black philosophy. The Black experience appears to be far from agnostic about love between men and women: on the contrary, it claims a profound knowledge of a condition that is considered by many to be as real as greens and hamhocks and as basic to existence.

The Black Soul may suffer deeply through love while continuously reaffirming it as a process: accordingly, all past love affairs exist and are transformed in the present. All men are potential lovers, all women are potential love objects. In this view, one may be unfaithful, while still being in love: the only real dishonesty is lack of love and the failure to admit it.

Given the frequent forthrightness of Black men and women in matters of the heart and their strong desire to find true love, it is not surprising that a life-time relationship between one man and one woman may be highly valued but difficult to realize. The process of loving may involve many partners, and although having children causes a woman to be more cautious and practical, it does not preclude a rich love life. More than one woman has given up security for love. When conditions prevent the ideal combination of lover and provider, a common solution is to keep the two matters separate, and to simultaneously maintain two types of relationships. The problem with this is that it may become a way of life, lessening a woman's chances of finding a satisfactory permanent mate. While marriage often leads to boredom, the thrill of a romance may cool off quickly when no commitment is forthcoming. The strongest commitment, but by no means the only one, between man and woman is to a home and family.

Lucille had never shared a commitment to her family with a man, although she regularly used all means available to her to gain support for her children. Even while she was working out her relationship with Sylvester, she was actively involved in various transactions with the fathers of her two children. When she broke up with Sylvester, the two of them had little to bring them together but memories; but she had good reason to keep in contact with the fathers of Arnold and Robert.

At first she had them imprisoned for nonsupport. She stopped this practice, however, because it kept the men from earning, but she steadily hounded them to do things for their children.

A "Would-Be" Pimp   Lucille had met Arnold's father at a girlfriend's house. Once she lent him ten dollars, which apparently excited him enough so that he told her friend he was "going to get every cent Lucille had." Since it was not any of her business, Lucille's friend did not tell her about it at the time. Nonetheless, Lucille caught on and whenever Lewison asked for a loan, Lucille claimed that she did not have any money. He told her that women usually do things for him, to which she replied that she was sorry, but if they were to keep on as they were, he would have to do things for her.

Some men are not above taking advantage of a woman's dilemma. According to a man's logic, if a woman sacrifices security for love, she can be persuaded to take the next step, which is giving money in return for love. A woman may fool herself about a man's love for her in order to avoid facing her problem squarely, with the man playing an active role in her delusion. The pimp is the professional at this, but there are plenty of aspiring amateurs.

When Lucille saw what Lewison was trying to do, she was able to deal with him effectively. During her pregnancy, she was very sick and almost lost the baby. Lewison said that he wanted her to have the baby. Subsequently, at the time of their break up, he threatened that he would not do anything for the child. Lucille then started, and won, a paternity suit against him, and since then he has been coming over to take Arnold to play with his other children, or they go shopping for clothing—anything to let Arnold appreciate some of the advantages of having a father.

After Arnold's birth, on several occasions Lewison asked Lucille to marry him. He felt guilty about his wife and children. Lucille knew and understood how he felt, because his wife was a good woman, who did not give him any problems and who stayed home with the children. But she was homely—she weighed about 250 pounds—and was not someone whose physical appearance he could be proud of. Appearances were important to Lewison, who was very dapper himself.

Male-Female Friendship: Lucille   Whenever Lewison came to visit Arnold, Lucille took great pains to avoid any situation that might cause him to try to renew their previous relationship. She was very friendly and talked to him about her problems with her oldest son's father and about things that happened at work. She would not discuss anything that pertained to her relationship with Sylvester, and quickly stopped any conversation in that direction. He sympathized with her about her first husband and gave her advice until she finally said: "Now don't let me get on *your* case."

Most of the men in Lucille's life came back to see her now and then; many seemed to be ready to take up again where things left off. It seemed that no matter how many women they were already seeing, they were always ready to take on another. Lucille was a challenge to them, especially to those who had stay-at-home wives: they felt that she needed a man who would take charge. Lucille steadfastly refused to let them do so, saying that they would have to put a lot more into her household before they could say anything about how she ran her life. Despite her rebuffs, they returned, enjoying her companionship and good-natured repartee. What they had achieved and shared with Lucille, or any woman, was always there; later experience could never erase it.

The father of Robert, her eldest son, called every so often. He was far behind on his support payments, but he did provide money for Robert's tuition and bought him clothes on special occasions. He was not selfish like Arnold's father was: if she asked him for twenty dollars and he had twenty-one, he gave that, whereas she considered herself lucky if Lewison gave ten dollars. While Lewison had a fine wardrobe, he would let his son go ragged.

Robert, Sr. criticized Lucille for having a man in the house while his son was growing up. He thought it was a bad influence on the boy. Lucille would not take this interference from her former husband; she pointed out that if he had done his duty by his son a long time ago, there would be no problem. So Robert, Sr. began a campaign to get on better terms with his son's mother. He called up one evening while Lucille's brother and sister were in town and asked them all out that evening. They met him at a tavern, where he introduced his current girlfriend. He foot the bill for everyone that night and Lucille was pleased, especially when her younger brother, Terry, started to compete with him. She enjoyed seeing men act like they were supposed to or, at least, as she felt they should.

When Robert's girlfriend decided to leave, he sent her home in a taxi. Lucille remarked about this afterward, saying that she would not have tolerated such treatment. After the girl left, Lucille and Robert sat together, flirted a little, and Robert jokingly said that if Lucille were not so hard on him, he would ask her to marry him again. It was a very pleasant evening.

A Basis for Domestic Relations: Harriet   Lucille, who had been deeply involved in her relationship with Sylvester, was now free; her friend, Harriet, who had been independent for many years, was now living with a man. She complained that it was just like having another child around the house. He helped her out financially and was a calm, self-contained person, but she had little confidence in him. She looked upon men as essentially helpless, lacking good sense and in need of guidance. Most of them had not been raised properly, she felt. Her mother and father had been together for many years, but her father had "run around" a lot while her mother had raised her family. She was very capable and brought in more income than her husband. He sometimes spent his money on other women, but his wife stayed with him and never strayed, although she complained frequently. He had the final say in the home, and Harriet felt that he kept her mother from getting things accomplished. Still, they had remained together.

Harriet often thought about her Cousin Theresa, who was married to a man who had a "woman for every night of the week." He had another family besides Theresa's eight children; whenever Theresa wanted her husband she called over at the other woman's house to see if he was there. She loved her husband and had resigned herself to sharing him.

Harriet's sisters and eldest daughter were happily married with husbands who stayed at home. She thought her sisters were dull and she viewed her daughter's apparent contentment with some apprehension. Still, she had to admit that these women appeared to be getting what they wanted and were advancing in concrete ways she could appreciate: a house, a fine apartment, a savings account. Alone, Harriet could not possibly satisfy her desire for beauty and security. Wisely, she decided to compromise and to throw in her lonely, wayward lot with that of a man, at least temporarily. Perhaps she could learn to accept some of those qualities which, in the men of her acquaintance, seemed backward and alien.

REFLECTIONS ON "MEN AND WOMEN"

The two women and their love affairs portrayed here are not typical, nor do matrifocal households predominate in Black communities. Accordingly, some of the difficulties encountered by Lucille and Sylvester in reaching an agreement stem from their unique situations; others are experienced by many Black Americans; some by only those in an urban setting; and some by those of a working-class status. Certain themes undoubtedly transcend the idiosyncratic: for example, the concern to reach a compact satisfactory to both parties before they make any commitments. Here, marriage is viewed as the social recognition of a satisfactory resolution of differences, rather than as the beginning of a socially prescribed relationship. Such an agreement may be difficult to negotiate when consanguineal ties—in Lucille's and Sylvester's case, mother-son bonds—are strong. Lucille's eldest son, resentful of competition, created difficulties in her household arrangements with Sylvester; Sylvester could always go home to his mother, who was caring for his small sons.

The importance of the economic transactions between men and women clearly emerges in the foregoing account. A satisfactory economic arrangement can transcend personal problems and survive "outside" affairs, while if there is a lack of agreement on finances, such affairs may be used as an excuse or reason to end the relationship. This is the case with Lucille, who decided that Sylvester would not reform.

While Lucille is perhaps more "ready" for marriage than her friend, Harriet, both are highly critical of men. Black men often have a reserve of strength that they express by *not* doing what is "expected" of them, in a society that they feel asks too much for too little. Since social expectations are often to the benefit of women, they are naturally critical of men who fail to meet them. Still, Black women fundamentally respect the autonomy of the man, and even in more conventional relationships, Black men and women maintain a strong sense of self and of their rights as individuals.

3 / Love child

Being a mother in Black communities is challenging at best; being a young unmarried mother is a trial. In order to develop a mutually satisfactory accommodation with a man, a young woman needs experience; she may, in the meantime, become a mother before she is socially mature. In fact, often the experience of motherhood is itself judged essential to becoming a woman. On the other hand, social fatherhood is not essential to becoming a man, while it is considered necessary to first attain manhood in order to be an effective father. These differences in cultural assumptions about men and women lead to recurrent themes in the dialectic of the man–woman relationship, concerning the irresponsibility of men and the demanding and complaining nature of women. Even though these myths carry a kernel of truth and are perhaps useful in instructing the young and in maintaining the male–female polarity, they obscure the real complexities of relationships between men and women and the ways in which they relate to children born of their union. As is evident in the following accounts of episodes in the lives of fathers and mothers, a young man may have to compete with an arrangement between a mother and her daughter, or between a girl and her kin group, as well as to resist pressures exerted by his own mother, in his attempt to be a real father to his child. Not until he is a grown man with other responsibilities, in many instances, is he called upon to be a father in the full sense to his children or, alternatively, a surrogate father to someone else's children. The role of father, like that of mother, is greatly idealized and is felt to require the mature faculties of the person.

MOTHERS AND DAUGHTERS

A Difficult Apprenticeship In the few years since it was founded, the Carrington Care Center for Unwed Mothers has counseled hundreds of young mothers-to-be of various ethnic and social backgrounds in Chicago. The Center provides medical care and psychiatric facilities for girls during their pregnancy; it also operates a school so that their education will not be interrupted. While recent changes in mores have resulted in some modifications of school policy, many high schools still will not allow girls who are pregnant, or even mothers, to attend classes. The Center maintains that unless these young girls receive help and guidance they may never finish school and are thus at a double disadvantage in taking care of their offspring.

In the course of my research in the Black community, I had occasion to contact the Carrington Center in order to interview some of its clients. Having experienced the narrow perspective on the individual in society taken by some makers of social policy, I wondered if the personnel at the Center had taken the opportunity to immerse themselves in the life of the communities they served—to become aware of the differences between their own values and those of their clients—before trying to guide those who were seeking help. The aims of the ethnographer are, traditionally, counter to those of the social worker: the former attempts to describe and understand people as they are while the latter tries to alter their lives. Still, social workers need knowledge of the social and cultural principles operating in a community in order to render effective service, while anthropologists should assume some social responsibility for the communities they study.

The "genteel" atmosphere of the Center office—far removed, both physically and socially, from the communities it served—did little to recommend it as a center of community service. As Miss Adams, the Research Director, discussed the activities and clients of the Center I strove to be impartial; but being more interested in the clients themselves than in its activities, I subsequently concentrated on interviewing a number of girls who had gone through the program, trying to see the Center through their eyes and abandoning any ideal of objectivity. It seemed necessary to learn about the experiences of young Black women before attempting to evaluate a program relating to them.

Among the six girls I interviewed who had been in the program, only one, Adrienne Vincent, was married and living with the father of her child; another, Lois, who had married, was separated and living with her parents. Adrienne was from a comfortably well-off family, Lois from a very poor one. The others, from varying backgrounds, were single and working or attending school, living with their mothers or parents. For all of them, their mothers were central figures in their lives. Miss Adams believed that the communication between mother and daughter was the clue to the girls' problems: thus, mothers who avoided discussing sex or who overstressed its dangers put their daughters at a disadvantage in dealing with their peers. I came to agree with the view that the mother–daughter relationship was crucial, but not in the way that Miss Adams proposed. It is doubtful that a mother has much control over whether or not her daughter becomes pregnant; other social and environmental influences, such as the influence of peers, are probably much more important. Where a mother's influence is critical is in how a daughter works out her subsequent situation: whether and when she marries, whether she continues school, and her attitude toward men and marriage. The most useful role of a social agency is to help her understand her situation and to offer her the means of working out her own solution, rather than to impose one. The young Black mother may have serious problems, but she is highly pragmatic and in a potentially powerful and valued position in her community.

Harriet Jones' daughter, Gwendolyn, became a mother before the Carrington

Center was founded. When Gwen found out that she was pregnant, in her senior year, she gave up school and married her child's father. She finished high school later, traveling a long distance every day to a school that accepted mothers as students. When she graduated, she was able to take a job in a bank and help her husband support their family, which by that time included a girl and a boy.

Gwen's upbringing had been quite different from her mother's; Harriet's mother, had avoided discussing sex with her daughter. She had kept a close rein on Harriet, not allowing her to stay out after dark or to associate with boys. Her father warned her about the dangers of socializing with boys, although he was not specific about what those dangers were. When, in her late teens, Harriet got pregnant by a man who worked with her father, her parents pressured the couple into marriage. But neither had been ready for marriage, and it was a brief arrangement.

Remembering her own experience, Harriet had brought up her daughter to be aware of the facts of life. She warned her about associating with certain girls who were "not nice" and told her to watch out for herself; otherwise, she gave Gwen a great deal of freedom. Gwendolyn had a mind of her own; she met Loren in the eighth grade and they had gone together since, although Harriet did not approve. She did not believe that a young girl should be so serious about a boy and tried to encourage Gwen to meet other boys: she should learn more about people, and perhaps she would find someone she liked better. But Gwen was satisfied and ignored her mother's advice. She did not want to have anything to do with other boys and was very careful about her actions and the way she dressed: she would not wear miniskirts, saying she did not want to "catch eyes." And Loren was a loner who did not associate with other boys or girls, either; he fell in love with Gwendolyn and she with him and that was that.

Harriet worked nights and she knew that Loren was coming over to see Gwen while she was at work, but she felt she could not stop it without alienating her daughter. When Gwen became pregnant, Harriet was disappointed; but when Loren's parents refused to give permission for the marriage, Harriet took the couple to another state where they did not need his parents' permission. She did not approve of the marriage, but it was what they wanted. It seems to have worked out, she thought, because otherwise Gwendolyn would have come back home.

Although she is an independent young girl, Gwen gets along well with Harriet. She remarked to me once, "I have the sweetest mother!" with an enthusiasm unusual in a very self-contained young lady. Her pregnancy grew out of a long-term relationship and was a sign that she was ready for marriage; she was absorbed in the task of gaining financial security for herself and her child. Later on, when she felt more secure, she might relax and enjoy some of the freedom of self-expression that her mother had urged upon her.

A Conflict of Generations: Rachel   All young mothers, married or not, desire security, but not all can achieve it equally. Since a girl is dependent on her own mother, the way she handles her situation reflects how her mother reacts when she learns of her daughter's pregnancy. Harriet was able to take it in stride; her own mother had been less flexible and had forced an unwanted marriage on her daughter. On the other hand, the mother of Rachel Phillips—one of the girls who had attended the programs of the Carrington Center—had reacted in fear ·and anger by chasing away all her daughter's suitors and by attempting to alienate her from men.

Mrs. Phillips was not prepared for her daughter's premature venture into motherhood; Rachel was her eldest daughter, and Mrs. Phillips, a young-looking woman, had restricted her daughter's maturation. She told her nothing about the physical processes of becoming a woman. When Rachel, at age eleven, mentioned something she had heard about menses, Mrs. Phillips' response was, "Where did you hear that stuff?" Until she was fourteen, Rachel thought people had babies whenever they wanted them.

Because of her mother's restraint on her development, seduction by a man played a crucial, if painful, role in Rachel's history. When she was sixteen, she met a young man who "psyched her out." He "spouted off" about Truman Capote and about virtue, which impressed Rachel, who knew very little about men. He attended the nearby Lutheran Church with his mother, who at that time was very nice to Rachel. She even invited her over occasionally for dinner. However, when she learned that Rachel was pregnant, her attitude changed. She refused to listen when Rachel attempted to speak to her. She would cut her off abruptly, saying, "You'll have to talk to the baby's father"; her son pretended that he did not know who the father was. Rachel felt that his mother instigated him against seeing her. Soon after she became pregnant, he went into the service. He did make one attempt to see her, but Rachel was not interested in seeing him. He never did see his child.

Rachel's first sexual relationship had not been pleasant; it had taken too long, and when it finally happened, there was nothing but pain. She did not even know when she was pregnant; she described her symptoms to her boyfriend, who made the correct diagnosis. Rachel then informed her mother, and Mrs. Phillips was very angry. She would not allow her daughter to have an abortion or put the baby up for adoption; she even went so far as to ask the doctor not to let Rachel give up the baby. She insisted that Rachel pay the consequences for her actions.

Rachel applied to the Center and was accepted. She was grateful for their help, but she felt they could have helped her more in getting along with her mother. Mrs. Phillips had always been strict with her daughter; she did not allow her to go anywhere with her friends or to stay out late. Once, when Rachel went to a party and stayed out until 2 A.M., she found herself in serious trouble with her mother when she got home. Her mother did not let her wear nylon stockings: the school principal had to call her to ask permission for Rachel to wear them to a dance. Any boy who called her got a "lecture" if her mother answered the phone.

Rachel was upstairs babysitting for her aunt, when her boyfriend came to visit her; her mother, hearing footsteps upstairs, called to ask what was going on. Suspicious at her daughter's quick denial, she rushed upstairs; Rachel's boyfriend escaped through the back door, but not before Mrs. Phillips called after him and shook her finger at him. She knew that Rachel was pregnant at the time, but she did not know that he was the father: she acted the same way to all the boys who came by, as well as with Rachel's father. It seemed as though she did not want men around.

When Rachel gave birth, her mother told her to stay away from "those people," meaning the father's family. She was determined that Rachel bear the burden herself, although neither she nor her daughter were in a position to take care of a baby. Rachel had suddenly acquired a great deal of responsibility; she had little time to be a teen-ager. She did not finish school, but took a job as a checkout girl in a grocery store. Her mother babysat for her granddaughter, Denise, but Rachel felt that Mrs. Phillips did not really take proper care of the child; she merely "watched" her. She envied her mother, who could stay home with the baby.

Mrs. Phillips had a baby herself, soon after Denise was born, and Rachel felt hostile toward her new little brother, Tommy. She resented her mother's apparent attempt to compete with her. Of Tommy she complained, "He is just like his mother; he never listens to anything anyone tells him." Turning to her grandmother for sympathy, she discussed her mother's "mean ways," and the old lady exclaimed that she did not know how her daughter got to be so hard!

Rachel left home once to protest her mother's treatment of her, but she returned when her mother agreed to let her come and go as she wished. Rachel agreed to pay 80 dollars a month for rent and to buy most of the food. Although she now respected Rachel's rights, Mrs. Phillips complained about two of her daughters and how she had to take "nerve pills" because of them. Rachel could not understand this. Rachel's youngest sister was now pregnant and having problems, but she was trying to finish high school and planned to marry. Certainly Mrs. Phillips could not claim that her daughters lacked a sense of responsibility. A young friend of theirs had had three children by three different men!

Since she was the eldest, Rachel suffered the most from her mother's unhappiness and self-doubt; she was able to make it a little easier for her sisters, because she understood the problems they had to face and was now somewhat independent of her mother. Rachel felt that Mrs. Phillips had not learned anything from her own experience; despite what her mother said about them, she knew her sisters were not bad: "It's just that things happen to people."

The psychologist at the Carrington Center advised Rachel that she had probably become pregnant in rebellion against her mother's authority and attempts to keep her at home. Rachel did not agree with this view: she felt that she was looking for love her mother could not give her. Rachel was looking for a man who could take care of her and Denise, so that she could stay home and bring her child up right.

Among the clients I interviewed at the Carrington Center, Rachel was in most open conflict with her mother; still, she accepted her responsibility and was making plans for the future. Although Mrs. Phillips was upset by her daughter's pregnancy, she did not try to deny it or to avoid the consequences. By keeping a tight hold over Rachel during a most crucial time in her life, Mrs. Phillips was causing feelings of anger and frustration in her daughter, which could lead, on the one hand, to bitterness and defeatism, or to an active solution of her problem. While she and her mother were interdependent, Rachel did not hesitate to express her feelings about her mother openly. She felt neither guilt nor unfulfilled obligations. In becoming a mother, she was asserting herself and working for a life of her own.

In her study of Black women (1971)[1], Joyce Ladner states that many young girls

---

[1] Joyce Ladner, *Tomorrow's Tomorrow: The Black Woman.* Garden City, N.Y.: Doubleday, 1971.

feel that having a baby is a girl's initiation into womanhood, and that this experience produces a strong individual.

An Attempt To Advise: Lois   Unlike Mrs. Phillips, Mrs. McCoy willingly helped her daughter move toward womanhood. She wanted her daughter, Lois, to develop a firm relationship with a man, even though the odds in the poverty-stricken, high-crime area where they lived seemed to be against this type of relationship. Lois, who also attended the Center School, was a quiet, stay-at-home girl, who never gave her mother any trouble. Then, at age 14, she met Dean, a brother of her friend's stepfather. At first they all just "fooled around" together—her girlfriends and their brothers, and Lois and Dean. They went out to Riverview Park to play ball; Dean always hit the ball toward her and in other ways indicated that she was "special." Lois once asked her mother's permission to go to the movies with Dean, and Mrs. McCoy stipulated, "He'll have to pick you up here: I want to see this Dean. He has to ask me if you can go, like things should be done." So Dean came, although he was shy and objected to Lois, "I don't know how to make no speeches: What should I say?"

After their first date, Dean and Lois went out frequently. Dean made a good impression on her family; he took Lois to fine places and her father said that Dean was a nice and intelligent young man. Lois did not know at the time that Dean was in a school for "dropouts"; she thought he was in high school. She found out later that he was in a trade school.

One of the cardinal principles among young Black men is to be secretive about their personal business, especially with young ladies in whom they are interested. They must feel free to maneuver and to manipulate appearances. To be "mysterious" is deemed necessary to a successful courtship.

Dean and Lois's romance was a long and complicated affair, with Lois's mother acting as advisor. Dean gave Lois a watch for Christmas one year and her mother insisted that she return it. She explained to Lois that when a boy gives a girl things he expects something in return. She had told Lois the facts of life, but she had never before discussed this aspect of the man-woman relationship. Perhaps she was subtly implanting an idea in the girl's mind. In this and in other instances, Mrs. McCoy revealed herself as a willing accomplice in the progress of Lois' and Dean's affair. While maintaining a pose of respectability (which, to be sure, sometimes tended toward transparency in the circumstances in which she operated), she nevertheless left no doubt in Lois' mind as to where she stood: firmly behind youth, love, and a rich sex life.

Dean asked Lois and her girlfriends to come over to his mother's house one day, and when they arrived he offered them a cigarette. Lois had never smoked; she did not know about the others, but they all acted as though they did it all the time. Then he offered them a drink: it was vodka. Lois said she liked it, although she had never taken a drink before.

The next day, Lois' counselor called her mother and asked why Lois had been absent from school. When Mrs. McCoy asked Lois about it, she replied that she had been in school. This was the truth; she had only missed one class period when they went to visit Dean. Her mother said she would check on her story, but she never did. Lois knew she would not; by telling a "white lie" she was really respecting her mother's need to maintain appearances.

On the next occasion, Dean asked Lois to come over by herself. She remembered what her mother had said and refused to come, saying, "I know what you want; I won't come." But he persisted in asking her until she finally agreed. She came home late that day and her mother asked her where she had been. She replied casually, "over at Dean's," and her mother, who seemed surprised, exclaimed, "You've been where?" However, she did not forbid Lois to go back.

The situation continued until Lois became pregnant. Then they decided to marry. It was Dean's idea, although neither of them really wanted to. Lois's mother said she was too young, but she did not try to prevent it, saying, "If I do, later on he's going to say that her mother kept me from having that girl I wanted." But both Lois and Dean were relieved when they discovered that she was too young to be married, even with her mother's permission.

Lois and Dean finally did marry, but they did not stay together very long. Throughout their subsequent troubles, Lois's mother was involved, talking to Dean, advising Lois, taking her daughter to the police when Dean threatened her. She became deeply implicated in their problems, and Dean blamed her, as well.

Mrs. McCoy was poor and had several small children. In her concern to do well by her daughter, perhaps she put too much pressure on the young couple, and unwittingly contributed to the explosive events that occurred when Dean and Lois found that they could not work out their lives together. It might appear that she tried to push her daughter into adulthood. Given the social environment in which Lois grew up, however, it is equally likely that she was merely trying to accept the inevitable gracefully and to help Lois meet her situation with some success.

A Generation Gap: Eloise and Lucy Lucy Carter, Eloise Carter's mother, is in some ways a less practical woman than Mrs. McCoy, although she has the advantage of a better educational and financial background than both Mrs. McCoy and Mrs. Phillips. She and her daughter have many disagreements. Eloise claims that her mother is too idealistic; she herself is rather matter-of-fact. Lucy is critical of her daughter for lacking self-discipline. Eloise is of the opinion that she and her mother "can't make it" living together, although they get along fine when they are living apart. But when Eloise tried to live by herself, she lost her job and had to move back with her mother. Later, Eloise again moved from their apartment in a middle-income project because she thought the rent was too high, and Lucy moved with her, explaining that she would move to her own place later. They moved to an old house that had been converted into a four-plex; Lucy's daughter-in-law, awaiting her husband's return from the service, lived next door with her children, and Lucy's aunt lived downstairs. While she claims that she does not feel particularly close to her relatives, Eloise has nevertheless remained in their sphere of influence.

Lucy Carter is a dignified lady, rather light in complexion, descendant of well-to-do landowners in Georgia. Her great-grandfather on her mother's side was a white Southern landowner who provided his "family on the side" with a generous amount of land. Lucy and her brothers and sisters grew up with considerable knowledge of their white relatives, although Lucy has lost track of them since.

As Lucy's brothers grew up and started their families, most of them moved to West Virginia where they worked in the mines. One brother died; some of his children moved to New York, some to Detroit, and some stayed in West Virginia. They all finished school and went on to college. Lucy attributes this accomplishment to the fact that they lived up in the mountains during their youth and had nothing else to do. Two of Lucy's brothers moved to Chicago after she settled there; upon her sister's death, Lucy's nieces and nephews came to stay with her and her husband. They too settled in Chicago and raised their families there.

Carter, Lucy's husband, died when her children were still young. She had to raise them by herself in a city about which she knew little. She has had many problems with the two younger children, and has consulted with social workers and psychologists. But these people could not take the place of a father. Whenever anything went wrong in the apartment building, it seemed that Ted was blamed for it. He became involved with the wrong boys; he was easily influenced because he was slightly mentally retarded. He went to stay with one of Lucy's nephews, and appeared to be keeping out of trouble.

Lucy and Carter had moved to Chicago because his family lived there and his mother had begged him to come back. Lucy had not wanted to move and still does not like Chicago. She misses the gracious, easy-going life she recalls in the South and the quiet of the country.

> I remember, there was a pasture near us that my grandfather was supposed to have, but he didn't want it. In those days people had those things (divining rods) to detect water. They found water in that pasture, and it was so clean and pure that they used it for medicinal purposes: they used to bottle and sell it. Then they made a swimming pool, and we used to say to our grandfather, "See, you should have that land so we could have a swimming pool!" The water used to be so clean and pure down there. Now, I don't know: we're over populating the earth and dirtying everything up . . .

Chicago is the essence of everything Lucy hates about the modern world.

Her father, a brother, and her mother's sister still live on the old homestead in Georgia, and Lucy visits there often. Lucy has a longing to own some of the old family heirlooms; the old lady has sold many of them "for a song" to anyone who wanted them. Only the Northern relatives who have had to give up that life seem to care about these relics.

These mementoes—lamps, bedsteads, and the other appurtenances of family life—cannot recreate the relaxed, genteel life Lucy knew in the South as a child, nor can they provide the security that land brings in an agrarian society; nor can her mementoes recall the strong gallant man who nearly worshipped his wife and children.

When they first moved to Chicago, the Carters operated a small grocery store on the South Side. They worked hard. Lucy's husband suffered a heart attack in his early forties. He left the hospital against the doctor's orders, because he wanted to see that his family was all right. He realized that they were not prepared to face the world without his protection. However, he died after only a few days at home. His family helped Lucy out in many ways, but her own brother, Peter, and her eldest nephew really came to the rescue. Peter came by nearly every day, and has helped Lucy with Ted and Eloise. Mainly, he fills her need to talk things over with a man. Lucy's nephew has taken over the responsibility of raising her youngest son, and on holidays she takes the place of honor at the head of his table.

Lucy realizes that her children need a father, but she treasures her husband's memory and will not let another man break down her reserve. She has kept many souvenirs of their life together: she especially treasures a piano which, one day, he suddenly painted red, without being able to explain why. Eloise said that she would get rid of all those things and buy new furniture, but her mother still clings to that part of her past, just as she recalls her childhood in the South with nostalgia.

Lucy kept the grocery store after Carter's death, trying to hold the family together. Eloise and Ted helped in the store and had very little free time; she attributes her later troubles with them to the resentment they felt about this. Like many parents, Lucy tends to look for excuses more than for reasons. She finally sold the store and took a job as a social worker for the Urban Progress Center, counseling high school dropouts and their parents. It hurts her deeply that her own children "dropped out" and did not finish school; she blames Eloise for "continuing to do what she shouldn't and not doing what she should." Eloise said she dropped out of school because she did not have the right clothes to wear, but Lucy realizes that if she really wanted the education, clothes would not have mattered.

Eloise had some problem at the Carrington Center and did not finish the program. When she had her second child out of wedlock, Lucy was aghast. She would not allow Eloise to bring her son home: he was placed in a foster home until Eloise married; otherwise, he will be adopted. Lucy would not think of letting Eloise try to bring up another boy as she did, without a father.

Eloise works in Youth Employment at the Urban Progress Center, a rather responsible position, which she obtained with her mother's help. Her personality contrasts with her mother's: Lucy is charming, conscientious and cooperative, qualities which Eloise does not always display; Lucy is cheerful and good-humored, but Eloise appears angry and sullen much of the time and is far less articulate. She is proud of her mother and respects her, as well, although she feels that her attitude toward city life is unrealistic. Eloise acts independently, regardless of Lucy's wishes. She knows her world and makes her way in it with the air of one who accepts things as they are, rather than worrying about how they should be. Lucy, she feels, lives too much in the past.

The Female Bond   The ways in which Black mothers influence their daughters vary; as with White mothers, the deciding factors are their own needs and experiences, as well as their own upbringing. Early pregnancy is not uncommon, given peer group pressures and socialization among young men, who are especially interested in "making out" with younger girls; some of them actually seem to regard it as a duty to remove a girl from her mother's influence and to help her become a woman. It is an accepted premise that men attempt to control women. Mothers try to protect their daughters from these influences, but ultimately they tend to accept the inevitable and to work within the constraints of their environment, to a degree that depends on their own sense of security. Whatever the situation, as shown by the relationships between mothers and daughters described here, the bonds remain strong.

Among the families I knew, only Harriet's mother insisted that her daughter marry or even expressed anxiety about her not marrying. Since that happened, over twenty years ago, there is an indication that mores are changing. The situation described by Rainwater no longer seems to hold.[2]

> Early marriage confers a kind of permanent respectable status upon a woman which she can use to deny any subsequent accusations of immorality or promiscuity once a marriage is broken . . .

Among these girls, the first experience with a man is a trial: if it develops into a more permanent affair, good; but if it does not, well, Mama is still there, and there is always another chance to find a man.

A WELCOME ADDITION

The Importance of Children   Legitimacy applies to parents, not to children. So goes the social commentary in Black communities. Children are desired; they are tangible evidence of manhood and womanhood and, therefore, of one's humanity. If one does not fulfill his responsibility to future generations, then one can expect little return from life.

When Lucille Foster discovered that she was pregnant, her pride received a blow; she had strong feelings against having children by different fathers. She needed special medical care in order to have a successful pregnancy, so she left it to the baby's father to decide whether she should have the child. Later, she admitted that she really wanted the baby to prove that she could still have a child. After she won the paternity suit against the baby's father, he asked her if it was really his child; she said, "If you don't know that, you can believe what you want . . . the main thing is, it's *my* child." Arnold grew up to be an engaging, bright little boy, and Lucille remarked, "To think I didn't want that child! He meets me when I come home with such love; he really makes me feel I'm wanted!"

Harriet Jones' children were all conceived out of wedlock, although she married Gwendolyn's father. Harriet could not imagine life without her children: they gave her stability, authority, and a purpose for living and striving. She sometimes regretted that they all had different fathers; but she was a grown woman and that was her own business. Her children were hers, and no one could take them away from her.

In the rather freewheeling life of the city, the process of working out a relationship with a man, or even of finding a man who is ready to settle down, may take a long time. At the same time, children are important to a woman, especially in the absence of a stable relationship with a man; she needs someone to care for and to hold on to! A husband is not necessary to have children, and children are important if a woman's life is not to be lonely and unfulfilled. Men may come and go; children remain.

[2] Lee Rainwater, "Crucible of Identity: The Negro Lower-Class Family," in *The Negro-American*, ed. Talcott Parsons and Kenneth B. Clark. Boston: Houghton Mifflin, 1965, pp. 160–204.

According to the Carrington Center report, however, a young unmarried Black girl may experience shame and guilt with pregnancy. There may be anger and shame on the part of her family, especially her brothers, who may take it as an insult that their sister has been "made a fool of" by a man. More importantly, her act may be regarded as selfish, since she is not prepared to take care of a child nor, in many instances, is the father. She has taken on the prerogatives of a woman though she is not yet one, forcing on her family the responsibility of taking care of her and her child, as well as helping her to attain maturity.

Since a girl knows that to be a woman is, among other things, to have a relationship with a man and to bear children, she may let herself be seduced in order to attain this status, while not yet possessing the necessary mental and emotional attributes. If she does become pregnant, she must depend on adults around her for help, both of a practical nature and in learning how to be a woman and mother. Nevertheless, despite its burdens and strains, the Black family is better prepared to handle the situation than is the average White family.

Despite initial similar reactions by parents, the situation for Black girls served by the Center is somewhat different from that for White girls, once the child arrives. Fewer Black girls put their babies up for adoption; there is pressure in their peer groups against it. Also, there is usually an adult female who is willing to take on a new young charge, since the rewards of being a mother are high among Black people. In Black families, the burden usually falls on the girl's mother, although other family members may also be involved. The adult female is prepared to take on the care of an infant, although she may not be willing to do so when her daughter forces the issue. But usually, once the child has arrived, her learned responses take over, and the respected and authoritative role of mentor is hard to resist. A new person has arrived, and there is the excitement of new experiences and discovery through the fresh eyes of a new life. Secretly, the grandmother may covet her daughter's situation, and the two may conspire to assign the role of mother, at least temporarily, to the older woman.

A Strong Interdependence: Eloise; Rachel   A teen-age girl is usually not ready to be a mother; she may not have finished school, or she may have to work in order to support her child. If she has not found a man, the demands of courting inevitably conflict with those of being a mother. The division of responsibility between mother and daughter may be relatively smooth, or it may bring about serious conflict.

Rachel, who by becoming pregnant, forced her mother to regard her as "grown," wanted to put her child up for adoption in order to have freedom of movement; she complained that her mother, who would not allow her to get an abortion or to give up her child, did not understand the problems of being a teen-age mother. Mrs. Phillips, a mother several times over, knew what responsibility meant; her daughter, too, had to learn to accept it. By her intervention, Rachel's mother put herself and her daughter into positions of strong interdependence; Rachel had to work and support herself and her daughter, and she helped her mother financially while Mrs. Phillips stayed home and took care of the child.

Rachel resented her mother's claims on her income and considered her mother selfish and irresponsible. Mrs. Phillips complained when Rachel gave money to her aunt and grandmother, but she herself spent money foolishly, Rachel felt. She bought things extravagantly; she bought several loaves of bread, which would get stale, while Rachel had to bring home the essentials her mother forgot. She thought of moving in with her grandmother, but she knew that her mother would give her a lot of trouble; Mrs. Phillips would "raise Hallelujah" if she gave money to her grandmother instead of to her. At one time, Mrs. Phillips threatened to move out, but Rachel said she did not think that would be so bad. It was all right to live alone, as long as you did not let some man take advantage of you.

Rachel began to think in terms of a future for her and her daughter and avoided the boys who were in her peer group, whom she regarded as "jive time" and pimps. She bought an expensive set of children's educational books and taught Denise to be polite and well-behaved.

Rachel and her mother both regarded their children as personal achievements, and the competition and hostility grew between them.

Rachel's mother and Lucy Carter, Eloise's mother, both derived financial benefits from their daughters' new-found responsibility. For years they had been supporting their daughters without a man's help; now their daughters were working and helping out. Lucy continued to work, but she split the rent and food costs with Eloise. Rachel and Eloise both moved out for awhile and tried to make it on their own, but each had moved back after a short time. They needed their mothers as baby-sitters and could not handle the costs of a household by themselves. The mothers and daughters were very dependent on each other, emotionally and economically.

Eloise and Rachel referred to their own mothers as "Mother," rather than as "Grandmother" when talking to their daughters: "Don't touch Mother's lamp." Eloise would sometimes say to Lenore, her daughter, "That's your mother," pointing to Lucy, but Lucy would object, "No, your grandmother." Eloise complained that her mother had spoiled Lenore from the day she was born, and the child confirmed her view, orienting her behavior toward her grandmother when she was home, crying and whining, as well as showing her affection. Lucy took pride in her granddaughter's accomplishments, exhibiting her achievements in nursery school to visitors; she discussed her behavior, and compared it to that of her own children. Still, the burdens of a growing young ego weighed on an older woman with many responsibilities. Lucy complained that her daughter spent too much time "on the streets," and sometimes did not even take the trouble to feed her own child.

After Eloise and her mother moved into the apartment next to Lucy's daughter-in-law, both doors were left open and the children ran back and forth between the two apartments. The daughter-in-law watched the children during the day; in the evening they often prepared only one meal between them. Since Lenore had begun to play with her cousins, problems of discipline arose, which Lucy was too tired to cope with in the evenings. She looked forward to the day when her eldest son returned; he would play with the children, but when he was ready to stop he would tell them to keep quiet and they would know he meant it. At the same time, she criticized Eloise's disciplinary methods with the children, saying that she was too harsh and often caused crying and conflict when she could settle things with a little care and consideration. Lucy herself tended to threaten, but seldom carried out her threats. This inconsistency led to a repetition of misbehavior.

Despite her problems with her grandchildren, Lucy did little to encourage Eloise to marry. Instead, she looked forward to her own son's return. If Eloise married, she would be independent of Lucy, and Lucy would lose her status as head of the household. Although she occasionally spoke of moving out and finding an apartment of her own, Lucy admitted that what she really wanted was a house for all of them, including her two sons.

A Strong Family Base: Adrienne   More fortunate than Eloise or Rachel, Adrienne Vincent grew up in a secure home environment and married the father of her two children. Before her marriage, she and her daughter Caroline lived at home with her mother, father, and little sister, who is only a little older than her own daughter. Because everyone at home called Adrienne by her first name her daughter did likewise; she called her grandmother "Mother," and continued to do so even after Adrienne's marriage, although she then called Adrienne "Mother" as well. Caroline, who was three years old, played with her aunt, who was five, her mother's cousin, nine, and some other cousins, aged four and two, respectively.

Adrienne married Caroline's father when the little girl was two years old. The couple moved into a four-plex owned by Adrienne's mother. They share the first floor with Adrienne's mother's youngest brother and his family; Adrienne's brother and sister and their families live in the two apartments upstairs. The children all play together, and all the parents babysit for each other. If it were not for the children, Adrienne says, it would be just like when they all lived at home with Adrienne's mother.

Adrienne's parents live in a townhouse not far from the four-plex; Aunt Lorraine, her mother's sister, lives with her husband in the adjoining house. They have often spoken of knocking down the wall between the townhouses; it seems silly to have to go outside to get to each other's places and even sillier when they call each other on the phone. The two sisters have always been close. Lorraine and her husband had no children, so Lorraine "spoiled" Adrienne and her brother and sister, by buying them things their parents could not afford. The two women also brought up their younger brother and sister when their parents died. Adrienne's mother feels lost since her brother, her son, and her two eldest daughters have moved out and set up their own households. She often brings her grandchildren and niece home to play with her own little girl, because she also gets lonely.

When Aunt Lorraine's younger sister (Adrienne's mother) came from St. Louis for a visit, many years ago, Lorraine introduced her to the commander of her husband's naval unit. Soon there was a second wedding, and the two couples have remained together since then. Both men bought taverns after they got out of the service and they prospered; brothers-in-law and sons-in-law help out in the taverns in their spare time. Lorraine is a practical nurse, but she also works in her husband's place of business occasionally, and Adrienne's sister works full-time for her father. It is a tightly-knit family group, which gives emotional and financial security to its members.

Adrienne met her present husband, Roger Vincent, when he was a lifeguard at the swimming pool near her house. He was attending college, and at first he did not want to marry until he finished school. She objected that it would be too late then for the child, but they continued seeing each other without marrying for a year after Caroline was born. He bought a bed for the baby and arranged for diaper service. Caroline stayed with Roger and his mother during the week while Adrienne was going to school and then Adrienne brought her home on weekends.

Adrienne thought it was not good for Caroline to be moved around so much and decided to keep her at her parents' home. She was aware that Roger's family had a history of becoming attached to their sons' children: his brother had taken his son away from the mother and kept him down South, where he was attending college. When Adrienne started going out with other men, Roger did not like the fact that his daughter saw them more often than she saw him. So he finally proposed to Adrienne, and she said, "Yeah," in an off-hand manner, thinking he was kidding her. When he bought the engagement ring, she still thought he was joking, but they were married soon after.

Adrienne's Aunt Lorraine wanted the couple to marry in the Catholic church that she attended, and she made arrangements for a priest to conduct the ceremony. But Roger's grandmother hurriedly arranged for a Baptist preacher, and they were married in Adrienne's mother's house instead. Roger's grandmother had paged his mother at the warehouse where she worked and where she had gone that Saturday to get supplies to paint her house; she returned and appeared at the wedding in an old pair of jeans. Adrienne's mother arrived when the ceremony was nearly over; she had been on her way downtown when they went to get the license and was just getting home. Everyone, it appeared, had a very casual attitude toward the wedding.

The minister, who "came from God knows where," Adrienne remarked, because Roger's grandmother never went to church a day in her life, was quite old; he kept losing his place and starting over again. When Adrienne's mother came in she offered him a drink: she did not know he was a Baptist and Adrienne's father, who loves practical jokes, had put her up to it.

It was really a strange ceremony, Adrienne felt, but interesting; she often says to her husband, "I wonder if it was real. . ." They held the reception two weeks later; they invited the priest, who teased them about not being able to wait to get married.

Although this varies among families, the relatively casual attitude toward the wedding as a social ceremony, contrasted with the importance of the funeral, seems to underscore the relative strength of consanguineal, at least, extended family ties. Yet Adrienne's marriage, supported by both families, appears to be stable, although both she and her husband maintain a sense of independence.

Roger and Adrienne have since had a son. But Caroline is Roger's favorite; she does not obey him. Adrienne believes that this may be because Roger lived with his parents when Caroline first knew him. When he asks her to do something, she just laughs; their son, however, does whatever his father tells him to do, although he is less obedient with Adrienne. Children, like adults, are definitely persons in their own right, and Adrienne upholds in both word and action their rights to be individuals.

Enter the Paternal Grandmother: Diana and Lois Like Adrienne, Diana Lawson is a client of the Center from a relatively affluent background; her boyfriend was killed in Vietnam before they could marry. They were very close—he was already like a husband—and Diana has had a difficult time recovering from her loss. Diana and his mother have developed a deep relationship, which she says is more like a sister-sister than mother-daughter relationship. The two of them sit together sometimes and "act like complete nuts." Diana's little girl spends a lot of time with her paternal grandmother, and "Sometimes," Diana says, "I wonder whose child it is, hers or mine." In Diana's family, as in Adrienne's and Eloise's, family role relationships are complicated by responsibilities taken by grandparents for grandchildren (See Chapter 4, "Reflections").

The paternal grandmothers of Adrienne's and Diana's children were greatly attached to their granddaughters; neither tried to gain control of their grandchildren, however, since the girls' families were capable of supporting the mothers and their children and able to back up the mothers' claims on their children. It was quite a different matter with Lois McCoy and her mother-in-law. Because of complications, Lois had to stay in the hospital for several weeks after Dean, Jr., was born; her mother brought the baby home, and Metrice, Dean's mother, asked to have the baby for awhile. Lois's mother agreed to this until her daughter was released from the hospital. She thought that perhaps Lois and Dean might want to get married. Later, when he was trying to get custody of the child, Dean said that Lois had told him when she was in the hospital that he could have the child, but she could not remember ever having said that at all.

After she left the hospital, Dean wanted Lois to move in with him and his mother; he said that her mother's apartment was too small and too cold, and that she would catch pneumonia. She stayed with them for awhile; but she did not get along with his mother, who was "bossy," and Dean was very difficult to live with. When her own mother moved to a larger place, Lois decided to take her baby and move back home. But Dean threatened her, so she left without the child, and sent the police over to get Deanie. Dean told the police, "She can't support the baby," but they said, "If it's your child, you'll have to support it anyway."

Dean's mother called up and said, "He didn't mean all those things," and Dean came over to apologize. But when Lois left him alone with the baby for a minute, he departed, and took Deanie with him. So she had to send for the police again, and things continued in this vein for awhile. Finally, despite their troubles, the couple married. Dean refused to move from his mother's house to a place of their own, because he wanted to save money. So Lois remained with her mother and attended school, while the baby remained with Metrice.

As a result of marriage, Dean was even more adamant about his rights over Lois and his son. He told his mother, "If I tell her to take off her clothes and walk down the street naked, she'll have to do that . . . she has to do whatever I say." He was angry because Lois wanted to live with her mother; he threatened to burn up her mother's apartment, as well as her sister's, which was nearby. When fires were actually started in the hallways of both apartments, Dean was brought in for questioning. Metrice came to the police station and said he could not have done it because he was somewhere else at that time, and thus he was released for lack of evidence. Later, when he pulled a gun on his mother, Lois, and his son, Lois was afraid to make a complaint, because she felt that Dean's mother would probably deny it. Certainly, little Deanie could not be a witness: he thought the gun was a toy. Afterward, Dean told Lois, "If it hadn't been for my mother, you'd be dead." Dean's mother assured Lois that Dean would not really do anything, but this was not very comforting.

Once Dean came over with some friends and demanded to see Lois; when her mother said she was taking a bath and could not see him, he began to curse her. His friends became embarrassed and started to leave. His parting remark was, "Remember, Lois has to go to school tomorrow."

Lois missed many days of school because of Dean's threats. Her friend who lived down the street called and said, "Dean is on the corner here, waiting," and Lois would not go to school. Her mother told her to go to school and to call the police if he tried anything, but she refused to go. Lois was reluctant to explain to her counselor why she had missed school, although there was a possibility that she would not graduate because of it.

Occasionally, Dean would suddenly, inexplicably, be very pleasant to Lois; he would take her out to dinner and the movies, just like old times. He bought her expensive gifts at Christmas and on her birthday: a sewing machine, a tape deck. But as time passed, he began to see other women and he told Lois he wanted a divorce. He moved from his mother's house and informed Lois, "I've got me a fine pad . . . a stereo that long . . . I've got all kinds of women—Black, White, Puerto Rican, and they've got ideas. They ain't no young-assed broads." He told her he was not going to buy her a birthday present because he did not know whether she would accept it. She felt rather sorry about losing him, because he was not really a bad husband; he worked every day and supported his wife and child. "If it just weren't for his bad temper!"

When Dean decided that he did not want Lois back, his tactics changed. Now his main concern was to scare Lois away from her child, to keep her from trying to claim him and to have her declared an "unfit" mother. Sometimes he would not let her see the child, and threatened her if she made an attempt to see him. If he was there when she visited Deanie, he might just say "hello" and go on into the next room; on the other hand, he might start a scene and begin threatening. Once his mother suggested that if he gave the baby back to Lois, the whole problem would be solved. Dean objected, "I'm not going to give the baby to Lois: that's my boy." Metrice replied, "It's her child, too: it's from her." Dean ultimately threatened, "If she takes it to court, she may get him, but I'll have him back on the same day, and Lois will be dead the next."

Throughout this period, while her son was threatening and intimidating Lois, Dean's mother appeared to be on Lois's side. When Dean brought a woman to her house, Metrice scolded him, saying, "See your son here, you're going to get him all confused, bringing women around here like that. He won't know who his mother is." She advised Lois against signing his income tax since he did not support her, only her child; he did not even pay Lois's medical expenses any longer, saying she'd have to pay them herself.

Lois began to have more and more doubts about her mother-in-law's good faith; she suspected she was aiding and abetting her son's behavior in order to keep the child. When she was planning to take Deanie to the circus with her sister and nephew, Metrice said she would have him ready, but when Lois called to say they were coming, Dean answered the phone and said that Deanie could not go. Sometimes Metrice acted as though she were afraid of her own son: she brought Deanie over for awhile, then said, "Well, I'd better get back home now; Dean will be over and he'll be mad." She was always careful to acknowledge Lois as Deanie's mother; sometimes she would spank him if he did not go right over to Lois, saying, "Don't you know your mother?" They all said to him, "Who's your mother?" and he replied "Lois," although Lois did not think he knew what it meant. But if Deanie was sick, Metrice called Lois right away, because the hospital requested the baby's mother.

Despite her assurance that she was merely taking care of the child, Dean's mother acted as though Deanie were her own; she got angry when people told her, "He's Lois's." She snapped, "He's *from* Lois, but he's still mine, isn't that right, Lois? If I'm his grandmother, he must be mine." Her husband said, "How will he know who his mother is. . ."

In a rare moment of insight and honesty, Dean admitted to Lois that he thought his mother was trying to use his son to make up for the things she did not do for her own sons. He said, "We would never have Christmas, never get no gift . . . it was just like any other day. She used to tell us there was no such thing as Santa Claus, that she was the only Santa Claus, so that took everything away from it." That year, Metrice took Deanie downtown to see Santa Claus. She asked Dean for money to buy a coat for Deanie for Christmas, and that was the only time he refused to give her money for his son. She bought the coat anyway, and he gave her the money later.

Lois's sister asked her if she wanted her child and Lois replied, "I'd just as soon let him stay there now, since I know I couldn't give him the things that he has there." Her sister then asked, "Then, what's all the fuss?" Lois explained that she did not want to take the baby away from Metrice all at once, but more gradually. The next time Dean's mother brought Deanie over, Lois's sister said, "That's Lois's baby; she's probably glad that you can give him some things she can't, but maybe she'd like to have her own child. Maybe it's good for a child to go without things sometimes and to be with its mother. . ." Dean's mother got angry at this, saying, "As long as I'm alive he'll get everything he needs; when I'm dead they'll let him do without, but not as long as I'm around."

Lois was glad of the opportunity to finish school, but she did not want to lose her child forever; further, she did not approve of some of the habits her son was acquiring. Dean bragged about teaching his son to swear and Metrice allowed Deanie to say things that Lois did not like to hear. She resented it when her mother-in-law told her to spank the child when he was naughty; she did not see him often and she did not want him to think of her as unpleasant. When she spanked Deanie, he ran to his grandmother, which made her feel strange. She missed Deanie and liked to talk about him.

By all appearances, Metrice was merely making the best of a bad situation for which her son was responsible: it was Dean who was the villain, bringing upon himself the censure of everyone. In his defense, it should be said that he was trying to be a father and a man according to his somewhat patriarchal ideas, playing a daring role in the face of powerful and conflicting maternal forces represented by

Lois, her mother, and his own mother, as well as against a legal system that he felt to be inimical to his interests. Dean felt that because he supported his son and saw that he was taken care of, he was entitled to have all rights over him; also, because he and Lois were married, he should rule her.

Lois's sister warned her that the longer she waited, the more it would appear that she did not want her own child. So Lois finally informed her counselor at school about her problems with Dean and her counselor asked him to come in to talk to her. He and Lois went to see her together; he accused Lois of being an unfit mother because she did not come to see her child. Lois told the counselor *why* she did not come—because Dean carried on so—and the counselor threatened Dean, "If Lois doesn't come to see the boy, you call me; if I hear that you jump on her, I'll have her take you through every court and get the child and everything else she can." After that, Lois saw Deanie more often, and it was then that Metrice started to bring him over to her house.

When Lois went to stay with her sister for a few days, she instructed her mother not to tell Dean where she was. Dean tried to get a warrant against her for desertion. He told the judge that no one knew where Lois was and that she had deserted her child. Realizing what he was trying to do, the judge called Lois's mother and left word for Lois; she went to court and the judge pronounced it an attempt at illegal custody of a child, saying that they had to take it to family court. A friend told Lois that she should go to the Legal Aid Society, retain a lawyer, and tell him everything. But the case was dropped, and the families continued to work out the situation in their own way.

Now that Lois had some outside help, Metrice's attitude changed and Lois saw Deanie at least once a week. Possibly, Metrice realized that the intimidating tactics were no longer effective; if Lois were pushed too far, she might demand custody of her child, and in such a case, Metrice certainly could not keep Deanie. It was best to let things remain as they were: Lois should finish school and find herself a job. Then they would decide who should take care of the child. Lois's mother felt the same way, thinking that things would work out and that eventually Deanie would come to know Lois as his mother. More importantly, in the meantime he was getting the best of care, and was certainly growing up to be far from a backward child.

IN SEARCH OF A FATHER

The Need for an Adult Male   People are not born fathers, any more than they are born mothers. But women are more immediately and irrevocably thrust into the maternal role than are men into the paternal; often a woman must actively recruit and even tutor a man into the role, although he will learn to be a father only by relating to his child. This involves time and energy, which many young men are unwilling or incapable of giving because of other pressing demands of manhood.

According to Miss Adams of the Carrington Center, girls who find themselves with an unexpected pregnancy may turn to their own fathers for help. Apparently, at that time it is felt that a man's help and advice are needed. A girl may reject her baby's genitor in a "fit of pique" even if the boy wants to acknowledge paternity. If she has a father to whom she can turn, she will lean on him; if she does not have a father on whom she can depend, she may look for an older man to take his place.

A man who occasionally dated Lucille Foster confided in her one evening about his daughter, who was 18 and pregnant. The school had called to say she was sick, and her mother asked him to bring her home. He asked Lucille for advice, and she gave him plenty of it. She told him that his daughter really needed him now, and that he should take her for a ride on Sunday and ask her to tell him about it. He should tell his daughter that although it is not the best thing that could have happened, she should get herself together now so that she could go on and take care of her baby. He should not try to force her into a marriage now. Perhaps she should take a course in practical nursing so she could take care of her child.

About three weeks earlier, Lucille's friend had told her how worried he was about his younger daughter, who was 16 and who stayed out late at night, going to all sorts of places. The older daughter, who was now pregnant, had always been where she should be. At that time, Lucille told him it was the eighteen-year-old he should be worried about, not the younger girl, since if she did all of those things she could take care of herself. Now, it seemed, Lucille had been right. Sometimes in order to be a good father a man needed to know a woman to whom he could talk about things he could not discuss with his own wife.

Lois McCoy's stepfather took the place of her own father while she was having troubles with Dean. When Dean was trying to persuade her to move in with him at his mother's house, her stepfather would not let her go, saying, "These niggers wrap a young girl up, then they can do anything. . ." When Lois and Dean decided to get married, he could not say anything. Later, when Dean was threatening Lois, he told Dean, "Remember, she has a father." Lois's stepfather did not really have much power in the struggle between, on the one hand, Lois and her mother, and on the other, Dean and his mother. But at least Lois knew he was there and that he cared.

Angela Martin and her little boy were living with her mother and stepfather also; she felt that they spoiled her little boy. When he was naughty—like the time he got his hair filled with wallpaper paste—Angela got angry, but her mother merely laughed as though it was not to be taken seriously. Her stepfather treated the children—his wife's, her daughter's and her niece's—as though they were all his own. He brought something home for them every night; if he did not, and one of them wanted something, he went right out to get it. When he was home, they ran to him and he listened patiently to whatever they had to say.

Angela's cousin had come to live with them upon her mother's death. She baby-sat with the children—Angela's little sister and son as well as her own son—while the rest of the family worked. Angela was carrying her share of the responsibility, but she was also having a good time, dating several young men. She talked about marriage, but not seriously. She said that her son's father was not serious and "had too much of the streets in him" for marriage. When he came to take his son out to the zoo or to his parents', she was on "pins and needles" until they got back.

Adrienne Vincent, like Angela, could depend on an adult male—her own father —to help with her children. Adrienne had not been in a hurry to marry, either.

She was "playing the field" until her daughter's father grew worried about losing his little girl and finally proposed marriage.

Adrienne's own father had quit school to go to work in the sixth grade, when his father deserted the family. When his mother died, he was forced to stay in the South long enough to work and pay for her funeral; then he joined the navy. He learned to cook in the navy; after he was discharged from the service he worked as a cook, although he did not like the job. He saved his money until he could buy a place of his own. He was always able to provide the necessities for his children and, as they grew older, he could do even more for them. After Adrienne was married, she missed living at home, where she got everything she wanted. Her husband quit school in order to support them; he drove a milk truck and worked for her father in the evenings. But it would be a long time before he could provide for his family in the way that Adrienne's father did, although the couple was living in a pleasant apartment at a reasonable rent, with Adrienne's mother as landlady.

The Problems of Social Fatherhood   Girls without fathers are at a disadvantage in making a place for themselves and their children; they cannot relax and enjoy carefree youth, but must be constantly thinking about the future. Lucy Carter's daughter, Eloise, lost her father when she was only nine; she had been the apple of his eye, and whenever she showed his picture she said, "That's my heart," with a glow on her usually unexpressive face.

The father of Eloise's daughter, Lenore, was going to college; his mother did not want him to marry and he asked Eloise to wait four years, until he graduated. But she did not want to wait that long, and she began to hate him.

When Eloise had her second baby, the mother of the child's father came to see her at the hospital and informed her that the father was married and had several other children. Eloise and her mother felt that she should not try to raise a boy by herself, because he would need a man to talk to now and then. So she put him in a foster home. She felt that her daughter needed a father, too, but most of the young men she met wanted someone to take care of them: she couldn't be bothered with them. She was going with a man in his late thirties, who was very nice and who was concerned about her children. She did not know whether they would marry, but he helped her out financially.

In Rachel Phillips' mind, her daughter's father was a "wrong dude," although she felt that her mother and his mother had both conspired to keep him from his child. She was also critical of her mother for keeping her father away; she felt that her little brother needed a man around so he would learn a man's role. Her own daughter needed a father, too, but any man she married would have to be so right: he could not say anything to hurt her, nor could he say anything the least bit wrong in front of her daughter. Still, she maintained, he had to be a man and be dominant. One of her boyfriends did not have any backbone in his dealings with her, she remarked. She could not marry him, since anyone else could walk over him, too. For the present she was just using him; he took her to see her grandmother, even other men, and he sat and waited for her for hours. He really "got up off the scratch," (was generous with money) though, she had to admit. He tried to kiss her once, but she would not let him. She had never seen quite such a fool. Rachel, who looking stunning in a long fall and silk hostess gown, was convincing as a woman of the world, and was not to be taken lightly.

Most of the young men Rachel met were not suitable for marriage for other reasons:

> I won't have anything to do with a man if he can't do nothing for me. They talk that jive: 'Baby you look so good'; I don't need that. These guys make $100.00 a week: that's nothing. Most of them, I can make more than they can. Then they want to borrow from me. That's not getting it. I've gone with some con men: They try to beat you out of money. I've known a lot of rich young men, mostly pimps, who ask you for money. I work hard: I'm not afraid to work. I can buy my own things; what I need is someone who can really do things for me . . . Love doesn't mean anything for me. I'll never marry for love.

If a man had potential, Rachel tried to help him out. "This one fellow is going to automation school and I'm encouraging him. If he gets through and does well, I'll try to get him. I let them know what I want: I don't jive. I'm not going to end up at the bottom of Lake Michigan." But so far, Rachel has not found a suitable young man to be a father to her child.

An Older Man   Rachel turned to an older man, Bradley, who was 56, and who wanted to look after her: "Maybe a father image," she said. He is a college graduate, very cultured and wealthy, with a "tough" apartment. At first she thought he was a "square" trying to be "hip," but then she fell in love with him. She liked the idea of just walking into something. "He made himself out to be stingy: nobody could get a cent from him and no one could walk over him." He always took Rachel to the fanciest restaurants and clubs: "He knew how things should be, how a dish should be prepared, and he would send it back if he didn't like it." But he was generous with Rachel; he always asked if she had food in the house and he bought her and her daughter whatever they needed.

Doubts arose in Rachel's mind. Perhaps this was too much of a good thing, and maybe if she married him, he would be stingy with her, too. Bradley's wife was leaving him for another man, just when he was getting a lot of insurance money for an accident. The side of his face was burned and scarred and he was old and not very good-looking, but if you love someone, that should not change anything. "I can't figure out what's wrong," she said. "She is leaving him for a man who's more of a woman. There must be something . . . His wife calls up there and I answer the phone; she just asks for him, she doesn't say, 'Who's in my house?' There's something wrong. . ."

Bradley wanted Rachel to finish school.

> "He's so nice; I can't believe anyone is that nice. I have to get to know him better . . . When I go over there, he waits on me; he always wants to know what I want for dinner. He buys me anything I want. *I* wouldn't kiss anyone's . . . I'd get dinner, but because I wanted to eat, too. Whenever anyone does things for me, I wonder what they want; I guess it's all because all my friends are always after something, they always have some angle. Probably, I don't trust him because I don't trust myself; I wouldn't do something for nothing . . ."

Rachel discovered that Bradley was jealous. He called her at home one time after she had left his apartment; she had not come straight home and her sister answered. When she got home she called him back and he denied that he was checking up on her, but she knew better. He had never called before because she usually left so late that he knew she was not going to go anywhere else. Another time, she went out with some friends and he saw her with them. She wanted to make him jealous. But he stopped seeing her. She decided to forget his shortcomings and started to plan how to get him back. She said, "I'm trying to keep my foot in his house: I'll get in if I have to put everyone down." She would not even introduce some of her friends to him.

"They'd be the type who might break into his house . . . These kids I know, they're the biggest thieves around. I wouldn't even go into a store with them, they might take something . . . He suggested having a party there, but I'd never do that. He has a bar there: they'd drink up everything he has. He's quite hospitable; they'd take advantage of that, and I'd feel so bad . . ."

When Bradley finally called her again, Rachel began to look at the matter more critically:

If this works out with my husband—I call him my husband—I'll go in there. But I don't like taking my daughter over there. He has two dogs and they lick her face. I don't like that. We sit and listen to music: sometimes he'll play Bach and Beethoven. I don't mind it, but I wouldn't put it on myself. I can't sleep over there: he'll always wake me up and ask me if I want to eat something. In some ways he's like a woman. Sometimes he acts like I'm older: his wife is 40 years old. He bought me a slip once, and it came down to here! I told him I couldn't wear that; he never buys things that are 'hip.' My mother says, 'I know you (after you marry) you'll want to go out and show off your clothes.' But I'm not going to stay home all the time. Oh, I won't miss my friends, dancing and having a good time. I've had all that; it's no fun, they're all after something. I don't dance anymore, anyway: I just watch.

Rachel was ambivalent about marrying a man so much older than herself, but she had been disillusioned about men her age. She would like to build something with a younger man, but lacked faith in her ability to do so. She recalled her Aunt Caroline who had left her husband while he was having difficulties; now that he was doing well he was remarried and she could not get her hands on any of his money. She knew it was possible to find a good man, but doubted that she would find one. In the meantime, she was ready to settle for "second best": a man who was much older and not good-looking, but who was well-to-do, generous, and cultured.

The "Outside Child": Lucille Lucille Foster realized the importance of a father; her own father had been very concerned about his children's welfare and she felt sorry that she could not provide her own children with such a father so that she would not have all the responsibility. When things got to her, she could leave and know that another person would handle them. Arnold, especially, desperately wanted a father. He was so happy when Lewison came to see him and took him to see his other children.

When Lewison had a few days off from work one summer, he took Arnold to stay with him at his apartment; he was not living with his wife at the time. But during his visit, Arnold spent one day at Lewison's house with his other children, and while he was there he fell off a merry-go-round in the backyard and gashed his head. Lewison called Lucille, who was home from work, and told her that Arnold was having stitches in his head; he assured her that Arnold was all right and that he would bring him home by five o'clock so that his mother could see for herself.

Lucille was worried; five o'clock came and went and still no word. She refused to call Lewison's house, because she still felt uncomfortable about her affair with him while he was living with his wife. Lewison had told his wife that Lucille would be terribly upset if anything happened to Arnold while he was there and that she had better see that nothing happened. Poor woman, Lucille thought; she must have been worried, too.

Lewison finally came and brought his teen-age daughter and his two sons along with Arnold. He felt guilty and was nervous about Lucille's reaction; he tried to disguise his guilt by making fun of her concern, imitating how she had acted when she heard about Arnold's accident. Lucille responded in kind: "That's probably the way *he* acted," and Lewison's daughter confirmed that he was shaken: "He just sat there and cried, 'I can't do anything right' over and over." She added that one of her brothers had beaten up the boy who made the merry-go-round go too fast and "hurt my brother."

Lewison left with the children; he was keeping Arnold with him, since he would be off work and could take care of him. After he left, Lucille observed, "I really don't like Lewison bringing his children here; and I don't like Arnold to spend time with them at Lewison's apartment. Their father doesn't live at home, and they may think I am seeing him. I don't like to be suspected of it when I'm not."

A Man's Influence Arnold worshiped his father, but he liked Sylvester, too. Actually he was happy to let any man play a father's role with him. Robert, Lucille's eldest son, was less outgoing and sociable than Arnold; he did not like any of Lucille's male friends except Lewison, who was careful to stay on good terms with him. At Lucille's advice, Lewison gave Robert money whenever he gave anything to Arnold. Robert especially disliked Sylvester, who had been the only man besides his father to stay at his mother's house. He did not see his father often, but the two agreed on their distaste for Sylvester's presence in his mother's household. Arnold wanted his mother to marry Sylvester; on this point, Arnold and Robert were in deep, irrevocable conflict. Arnold sought a father, creating one where he could; Robert, being older, resented any man who might take a permanent place in his mother's house. Robert himself would soon be the man of the house, although he would never have much authority there.

Because of a woman's problems in dealing with a man, it sometimes appears that children are more concerned about having a father than their mothers are about providing them with one. To have a man in the house considerably lessens the authority of a mother who is used to running things as she sees fit, although, if he is responsible, he helps to lighten the burden.

Harriet Jones' daughter, Gwendolyn, kept in touch with her father, although Harriet had long ago lost contact with him. Her son, Daniel, asked what his father was like: he had never seen him. Harriet tried to look him up once, for Daniel's sake, but she could not locate him. She felt that her children did not really need a father, because men did very little about raising their children, anyway, leaving everything up to the mother. Still, when she began to share her apartment with an old friend, she was happy that the children had someone to help them with their homework and to talk to them. Sometimes her children annoyed her. At those times, it was good to have someone there to calm her down and to take care of the children. And Daniel and Carla seemed to appreciate him, too. They settled down quickly and willingly to life with a man in their home; with all the canniness of the young they recognized in him a friend and ally.

A man, most women and all young children feel, is good to have around the house; but when the chips are down, Mama is always there, while Papa may be off somewhere chasing a rainbow.

REFLECTIONS ON "LOVE CHILD"

In important human relationships requiring some regulation—as between parent and child, husband and wife—Black Americans may not accept the terms and decrees of a legal system designed for a conjugal family system, in which parents take all responsibility and have sole rights over their children, and a man is the sole support of his wife and children. These requirements do not hold in the case of extended families, where grandparents, aunts, and uncles share responsibility for children and in which a woman may receive support for herself and her children from sources other than a husband and father. Each situation is somewhat different; therefore a working agreement must be reached in each instance using any means at hand, ranging from reason and promise of reward to threats of external intervention, even of violence. In these informal legal procedures, the legal system may be used as a means of enforcement rather than as a final authority because it is not responsive to some of the values and needs of the contending parties. These methods are used by Lucille in dealing with the fathers of her children, by Lois and Dean, and by Adrienne (although the latter relies mainly on persuasion). Harriet and Eloise, who show ambivalence toward men in general, are less involved in such activities at the time of this report; neither has been markedly successful in previous efforts.

Marriage is not necessarily a solution for the problems of a young unmarried mother, as Lucille advised her friend, the father of an unmarried mother-to-be, and as Lois discovered with Dean. Reaching an agreement between two people with prior obligations is difficult enough; a third party in the form of a dependent child introduces additional complications. If a father admits paternity (and apparently this depends to some extent on the actions of a girl and her mother) and accepts responsibility, the respective rights of the parents must be worked out; and if the two are young and dependent on their families, the rights of other family members must be considered as well. Thus, Lois's mother-in-law asserted her rights over Deanie, whom she said was merely "from Lois," which indicates a separation between social and biological concepts of descent and parenthood that is not characteristic of European-based societies. Furthermore, it is recognized that time is needed to develop the capacities for parenthood, which do not automatically result from either a biological event or a social ceremony.

In the matrifocal families in this study—Rachel's, Gwen's, and Eloise's—mothers made little attempt to establish contact with the father of their daughter's child or with his family, and they did not encourage their daughters to marry. This led to strong interdependence between mother and daughter, for Rachel and Eloise in particular; both girls turned to older men in search of security. In the conjugal households of Lois, Adrienne, and Angela, on the other hand, the young fathers became involved with their children and Adrienne and Lois married their children's fathers. In these instances, a structural continuity between families of orientation and families of procreation seems to exist, with matrifocal households giving rise matrifocal households and conjugal households to conjugal households. This may reflect a difference in bonding patterns, i.e., female-female as opposed to male-female.[3] However, these situations may be temporary: the recording of the temporary cycles of many households over a long period of time would be necessary to form such a generalization.

The wishes of the young parents and the relationship between them also play a role in the eventual settlement: thus Gwen determined to marry despite her mother's disapproval; Angela felt her young man was not ready to settle down, although she granted him visiting privileges. But, in any case, the child, who is the occasion of the plans and programs, is taken care of and the mother is on her way to being a significant force in her family and community.

[3] See Lionel Tiger and Robin Fox, *The Imperial Animal.* New York: Holt, Rinehart and Winston, 1971, Chapters 3 and 4.

4 / Save the children

INTRODUCTION

Black mothers are strong and protective. In the communities in which they often must raise their children, these are necessary, socially approved traits. They impose strong discipline because a child needs to learn respect for others and for social order in an environment where chaos and anarchy are daily threats. They surround their children with a network of family and friends, furnishing them with a sense of security and sensitizing them to social values. Contrary to some beliefs about Black children raised under these conditions, they develop a strong social identity.

MAMA'S CHILD

Lucille and Rosalyn: Protection or Overprotection? On Chicago's South Side the character of neighborhoods varies radically from North to South and from East to West. The Northeast end is dominated by the imposing luxury apartments of Lake Meadows and Prairie Shores; immediately south of the Lake Meadows shop-

High-rise, low income housing

Homestead (suburban)

ping center are low-income Housing projects—high-rise buildings and row upon row of six-unit dwellings, crowded together, with a small park accommodating all the children of the Projects. There is only one small swimming pool, but in the summer the police turn on the fire hydrants and scores of the smaller children run shouting through the chilly spray.

Between 39th and 50th Streets is a vast wasteland of dreary, dilapidated apartment buildings relieved only by the large, comfortable stone houses lining Martin Luther King Drive and Drexel Boulevard. In the worst section of this neighborhood, lives Lois McCoy. It was here, in the summer and fall of 1969, that there was a rash of fires. Whether it was the work of an arsonist or merely an eruption of pent-up anger in the heat of the summer was never discovered.

From 50th Street southward for about ten blocks and west from the lakeshore to Cottage Grove is the enclave of University intellectuals and middle- and working-class Black families known as Hyde Park. An underlying current of fear exists in this neighborhood, as though the misery to the North and South might overflow into its streets. To the south is the territory of the Blackstone Rangers and Disciples, where life is problematic for young boys on the streets. Rachel Phillips and Lucille Foster live within this area, fearing for the safety of their children in a neighborhood where there is little time for childhood. Earline, Lucille's "adopted" sister, lives in the relatively exclusive South Shore district to the East, but her son, who is in and out of trouble, has not escaped the many traps set for the young on the South Side.

Townhouse

Lucille Foster has kept her son, Robert, off the streets by means of strict rules; she does not allow him to go out in the evenings except on special occasions. Although Robert is a withdrawn and quiet youth, she does not regret her policy in the least. When Robert was fifteen, she attended the funeral of her Cousin Delores' son, a seventeen-year-old who was shot while trying to rob a grocery store. He was with his older brother, who was arrested for armed robbery and attempted murder.

Lucille thought it must have been his brother who got the younger boy into trouble; the older boy had been arrested many times, while the younger one had been Delores' "best child." Lucille remembers him as a little boy: "He used to deliver groceries on 63rd Street when he was eight years old. He bought a red wagon and two batteries; he used to start people's cars when it got cold, picking up 4 or 5 dollars. He'd never been in trouble before. . ." Aunt Lily said she had seen a man pick the two boys up at eight o'clock in the morning and by ten he was dead. She called Lucille and said, "Delores needs you right away," and so Lucille went. It was really a terrible thing! Someone said to Lucille, "He shouldn't have been trying to rob a store," but that was not the point. It was terrible that a boy who had not begun to live was now dead.

Two years prior to this event, Delores had put her son into a different school because the Blackstone Rangers were trying to get him to join. It did not seem to matter, however; if a boy was pointed toward trouble, he could find it anywhere, especially on the South Side.

Cousin Delores was married to a man who mistreated her; she would at times neglect her children in order to keep up with his meanderings. He once wanted her to go to Detroit with him, and she reluctantly agreed, although she had to miss her son's graduation from grade school. Lucille said, sadly, "It's too late for her; she just doesn't realize she could be treated right: men have really abused her." Delores is somewhat unstable and has spent time in a mental hospital. After her release, her older boys have on several occasions saved her from severe mistreatment by her husband. But worst of all, from Lucille's point of view, her problems have kept Delores from being a strong mother—a real tragedy for young Black children in the city.

Death is no stranger to children growing up in South Chicago. Shootings, knifings, and other types of violence in gang shoot-outs, robberies, or just fights often result in fatalities; illness also takes a heavy toll. Lois McCoy and her friends attended a wake one evening for a boy who was shot by his brother; she did not know whether it was an accident or the result of an argument. A few weeks later she attended another funeral for a classmate at the Carrington Center, who had died of pneumonia; her own sister died shortly thereafter of a brain hemorrhage.

In the high-rise Projects, the perils of the streets are brought into the hallways and elevators, which are the scenes of assault, rape, dope peddling, and other activities dangerous to residents. Even little children are not safe: the body of a seven-year-old girl who had been raped and stabbed was found on the elevator in one of the Projects.

For some time, Rosalyn Martin had been trying to move from a high-rise project; she worked every day and had no car, so she had little time to look. Also, it was difficult to find a place she could afford that was large enough for herself and her three children. By working hard and long hours as a key-punch operator, she was able to feed her children and keep them well dressed, but she had not been able to provide them with the kind of home environment they needed.

Rosalyn's teen-age daughter, Linda, hated the Project; she ran away from home and moved in with a girlfriend who lived with her mother, a white woman, in a luxury hotel on the lakefront. Rosalyn was hurt by Linda's leaving home, but she felt that she was probably better off at her friends' for the present; she increased her efforts to find an apartment. She finally located a small house at a reasonable rent, paid the woman a month's rent, and prepared to move. But when moving day came, Rosalyn found that the woman had not moved yet and further, that she did not even own the house. Rosalyn brought the police and got her money back before the woman could leave town. But she was still without a place to live and had to resume her hunt.

Meanwhile, Linda was enjoying her stay at her friend's house. The girl's mother, Mrs. Watson, let the girls go out by themselves and entertain their friends at home. At her mother's, Linda had little brothers who got in the way and her mother would not let her go out by herself or bring her friends home when she was not there. At Mrs. Watson's, Linda's social life improved. Dressed in "mod" fashion, with dangling earrings and Afro hairstyle, she was becoming quite a young lady. She never wanted to return to the Project, where her life was so restricted.

When Rosalyn visited Linda, Mrs. Watson told her, "You don't give Linda enough freedom to be herself; she is suffering from overprotection." Rosalyn only looked at Mrs. Watson across a vast gulf; she wanted to reply that it was only because of her "overprotection" that Linda had not been caught in the hopelessness of her surroundings. When Rosalyn finally did find an apartment, Linda moved back home and was extra sweet to her mother, trying to make up for hurting her. She helped her out in many ways to show how much she appreciated her, even though she had had to leave home temporarily for her self-development.

After she moved, Rosalyn missed certain things about the Project, especially the freedom her boys had to come and go. Her new landlord did not like children and did not hesitate to let her know it. The boys' activities were considerably restricted and he constantly complained about them. Gradually, however, the boys grew used to the landlord's requirements, and Rosalyn came to appreciate the relative peace in the neighborhood.

Jeanine: Toward a Better Environment   At about 90th Street South is a section of new houses sold to refugees from areas to the North. While they cost the residents dearly, these houses begin to fall apart when they are only a few years old. Jeanine Smith and her husband bought a house here in order to bring up their children in a pleasant and safe neighborhood. Jeanine had spent part of her childhood in the Mother Cabrini Greens, a grim high-rise project on the near-Northside where intimidation, rape, and even homicide are facts to be lived with. Jeanine's husband was a draftsman for an architect's firm, and Jeanine worked as a secretary. Her husband's parents and brothers came to live with the couple when they bought the house, and the boys helped to meet the high monthly payments.

The families in Jeanine's neighborhood who had bought their houses on contract began to see that they had been grossly cheated. Screens and screen doors that had been promised never arrived, paint peeled, plumbing and heating systems failed, and houses began to reveal shabby workmanship throughout. They felt that this happened because of their lack of money and experience, as well as because of the limited number of good neighborhoods into which they could move. The families banded together and formed the Contract Buyer's League, withholding monthly payments and putting the money in escrow instead. They demanded a reduction of the contract cost to an amount nearer to the estimated value of the houses. Jeanine became one of the most active members of this group, changing almost overnight from a fairly quiet, conforming young woman to a vocal and active militant.

The reaction to the activities of the Contract Buyer's League was predictable and swift; soon there were newspaper articles and pictures of families and their belongings out in the snow. Scores of police dressed for combat, and even helicopters, were sent to evict ordinarily peaceful citizens from their homes, showing that it was hopeless to try to escape the consequences of growing up poor and Black in Chicago. Some of the members capitulated and paid up, while others became more determined. One man even threatened to protect his family and property with a shotgun. Jeanine was "radicalized" in a confrontation with a sheriff's deputy, who she said acted like a "storm trooper"; for the first time, she had a gun pointed at her head. She became more adamant about gaining just rights for herself and her family.

Publicity brought much support and sympathy for CBL, but the evictions continued. As a result of withholding payments over a period of time, however, some of the Buyers were able to make a downpayment on more suitable property elsewhere. Jeanine and her husband bought a well-built duplex in the South Shore district, where they became landlords. They enjoyed their new status, sometimes joking about being hard on their tenants, who were white.

Problems at School: Rachel The greatest fears of Jeanine and other parents were of the perils lurking in and around public schools in some Black neighborhoods. There, gangs attempted to recruit and intimidate the young, sometimes even killing them if they refused to join. Rachel Phillips, who lived in Blackstone Ranger territory, was worried about sending her daughter to school when the time came. Things used to be so different when she was in school; now her little brother came home talking about "P-Stone" (Blackstone Rangers), how they took the kids' lunch money for protection. And he was only eight years old! If anyone terrorized her daughter, she would "whip them!" she threatened.

Things were really changing. Her mother used to leave her door unlocked; now, even when she was home, Rachel kept the door locked. She never answered the door without asking who it was, even if she was expecting someone.

Things were stolen at school. The attitude toward education was also changing. When her mother and aunt went to school, there was no stress on clothing; you could feel accepted no matter what you wore. You were in school to learn as much as you could. But now, even in the better schools, there was little respect for education. She had so much respect at first for the high school she attended; it boasted a good reputation. But she did not learn anything there, other than how to get along here in the world and how to cope with people. That was not what she meant by education. It seemed like the kids just went there for fun, and even the teachers did not care. Her Aunt Caroline said that she had been really interested in school, and that there were many new and interesting things to learn nowadays, too.

When Rachel attended school at the Carrington Center, she did much better than she did in high school; she thought maybe it was because there were only girls in the class. She wrote an analysis of "Prufrock," which her teacher said was better than many essays written by college students; Rachel had worked for weeks on that. Perhaps she was thinking about Bradley when she wrote it. But after she had Denise, Rachel was not able to even think about finishing high school. Now she thought about her daughter's education and future.

Most mothers rely on discipline as most effective in protecting children from their environment; eventually, the theory is, imposed discipline becomes self-discipline. Harriet Jones and Lucille Foster both sent their children to parochial private schools, in order to keep them off the streets and because they would learn better discipline than in public schools. Lucille and Harriet were both brought up as Baptists, but as parents of parochial pupils they were required to attend Mass and to be active in school activities. Although Lucille eventually became confirmed as a Catholic, Harriet remained a Baptist; and both of them shared some philosophical differences with the Church. Lucille could not agree with the rigid views of the Church on marriage and sex; Harriet could not accept the concept of the Virgin Birth. Nevertheless, they both were keenly aware of the importance of religious values as well as the advantages their children would have in being educated in a private school.

Holy Angels, the school that Harriet's children attended, is a progressive parish servicing the entire area of the Ida B. Wells Project. Most parents in the Project try to scrape together the modest tuition fee to send their children to school there, so the enrollment is high and classes are relatively large. The head priest is Black, and in Sunday School and day school children are taught to be proud of their Black

Palm Sunday procession *Holy Angels church*

heritage. In August 1969, a new and innovative ordaining ceremony for three new Black priests took place at Holy Angels. The opening procession revealed the three novices wearing African robes, four policemen from the community—one White, three Black—and other priests and church officials. The chancel was decorated with African art objects, as well as the usual religious paraphernalia. The head priest gave a militant sermon, which was quite long. Harriet decided to leave in the middle of it, because her children were sleepy and "fussy."

Harriet: An Issue of "Class"   Although her children were learning to be proud of their Black heritage, Harriet sometimes did not share that philosophy. When she took her children to the lakeshore, which she often did in the summer, she did not

---

MASS OF BLACK UNITY

&

SOLEMN INSTALLATION SERVICE

The 12:15 Mass today is a special Mass concelebrated by some of the Black priests of Chicago and other parts of the country, to celebrate the naming of three black pastors of Catholic Churches in Chicago's Black Community.

WE CONGRATULATE--

Fr. George Clements: pastor of our own parish, Holy Angels

Fr. Dominic Carmen: pastor of St. Elizabeth parish

Fr. Kenneth Brigham: administrator of Our Lady of Perpetual Help

WE WELCOME--

All the visiting priests from Chicago and from other cities who have come to join in the celebration.

All of our visitors, clergy and lay people from the Catholic community and from other Churches.

WE THANK--

The women of the Blessed Sacrament Society of Holy Angels for serving at the reception after 12:15 Mass.

The musicians and choirs who help us sing praise and thanks to God.

Everyone else who has worked to make this celebration possible.

*   *   *   *   *   *

The Concerned Black Christians will hold a celebration party for Fr. Kenneth Brigham this Tuesday evening, July 1, at 7:00, at St. Mary's High School, 2044 W. Grenshaw. Everyone is invited!

care to go to the "Point" because too many of "our people" would be there. She guessed she was prejudiced, but she did not like to be around her own people too much because sometimes they did not know how to behave.

Harriet shared with others of "her people" the bias against dark skin. She herself is dark-skinned; her two daughters are light-skinned, while her son, Daniel, is even darker than she is. She was also critical of "her people" as parents: the men generally did not take an interest as fathers, she felt, while the women were often ignorant and did not raise their children properly. She criticized the woman who lived upstairs, the mother of the young man she had gone with, for not teaching him to respect women. Often, too, children were left to fend for themselves. A distant cousin who lived in the Project had been left with her younger teen-age brothers and sisters when her mother died. Her niece came to live with her, too, as well as the man the younger girl later married. It appeared as though the kids just "took over." Harriet's eldest daughter used to go over there, but Harriet stopped that.

Harriet was appalled at the way families were living "crowded up" in the projects; as families increased they did not move to larger apartments, but merely doubled up in the two bedrooms. One family had two teen-age sons and two teen-age daughters with only two bedrooms. Another had a teen-age boy who slept on the sofa and four or five small children who shared a bedroom. Her son, Daniel, was now ten years old; she felt he needed a room to himself, since he was too big to share a room with Carla. This, along with her desire for a nicer place, was her motive for moving to the medium income apartments, though she really could not afford it. Harriet aspired to a better way of life.

Harriet and Lucille: Problems of Working Mothers   Harriet wanted to have the best for her children, but she determined not to overprotect them as she felt her parents had overprotected her. Because they had both worked, they had hired an elderly lady to take care of her; she had been afraid of what might happen to Harriet and would not allow her to go anywhere or to have any of her friends come to her home. Harriet listened to the radio frequently and as she grew older, she spent much of her time in church. She went to church nearly every day, as well as on Sunday. She also spent hours in the playground, playing volleyball. After she started high school, she was able to play in the playground until "dust dark," when she had to come home.

Harriet's cousins had much more freedom than she did. They did not like to come to her house because of her father's interminable lectures. He would lecture to the girls for hours about the evils of the modern day, and they would soon grow bored. Their mother was away much of the time and they would slip away to the South Side to have some fun. But Harriet would not go along; she knew she would get into trouble with her parents, and besides, she felt uneasy around the boys they would meet. Her father had been especially eloquent on the subject of boys and the bad things they could do to young girls. Later on, when Harriet and her sisters started to date boys, he cornered their dates and lectured to them until there was hardly time left for the date. He even threatened them with a gun sometimes, although Harriet thought he really did not mean it.

When Harriet became a mother and then began to work, she left Gwendolyn with a couple who were distant relatives; they were very congenial people and were kind to Gwendolyn. But they both died. When her two other children were born, Daniel and Carla, she left them at home with Gwen. She did not trust anyone else with her children. Besides, she would have to keep her clothes and her phone locked up, even with an older person, and she did not want any man around the house, especially with a teen-age daughter.

When Gwen was married, Daniel was only seven and Carla was three. Harriet decided to leave them alone when she worked at night, although she was worried at first. She gave the lady downstairs a key in case of fire; she was home all the time. Also, she was "nosey" and saw anything that happened, and her boyfriend was there at night. Harriet trusted to the Lord and decided not to worry; but she had the locks changed and a chain put on the door when it was reported that someone had gotten hold of a passkey to the apartments.

Daniel called Harriet if anything was wrong; sometimes, Carla got sick and ran a fever. The next door neighbor heard her wake up crying and told Harriet about it the next day. But Harriet told Daniel what to do. She had medicine there at home and gave him directions about what to give to Carla. Sometimes they got "six bells"—a childhood digestive ailment. Harriet was defensive when people spoke to her about Daniel and Carla, saying that she could not worry about her children.

Carla's health was always rather shaky, although she did not have anything serious until she was six. She had a lingering cold all winter and Harriet tried to keep her wrapped warmly when she went out and gave her home remedies. She still worked nights and got home in time to fix the children's breakfast and send them off to school. But Harriet's home remedies, though more sophisticated than most, did not work once, and Carla's temperature kept rising, up to 104°. Harriet gave her a shot of penicillin that she had brought from work, but Carla broke out into a rash and her temperature remained high. Finally, she took Carla to the doctor and discovered she had the measles. Her friend Lucille was critical of Harriet for giving Carla penicillin and for not taking her straight to a doctor. Harriet felt she had to be everything to her children, but even an RN could not give medicine without a doctor's prescription, and Harriet was only a LPN.

Carla's resistance was now down, and she contracted pneumonia. Again, Harriet tried to nurse her child herself, but when she detected trouble in Carla's breathing, she finally took her to the doctor. Carla had a collapsed lung and had to stay in the hospital over Christmas. Harriet wanted to bring Carla home for Christmas since she had improved greatly, but the doctor would not allow it. Again, Lucille was critical of Harriet for wanting to bring "that sick child" home. But Harriet felt that home was the best place for her child.

After Carla was released from the hospital, Harriet held a birthday party for her, with decorations, favors, balloons, and hats for everyone. She often remarked that one of the good things about the Project was that whenever she wanted to give a party she could go out in back and just "grab a handful of kids." She took pictures of the children, then of Carla and Daniel alone, after all the children had left. Carla stood stiffly, not knowing what to do with her hands. Harriet tried to pose her, but then lost patience. She told her to relax and keep her legs, which were slightly bowed, together. She got out some pictures which she had taken of Carla in her hospital bed and showed them to me; I had arrived just as the other children

Birthday party

left. Harriet was determined to record every facet of her children's life and to put her own mark there, clearly.

Harriet believed that her children should learn responsibility early in life; then they would not have so much trouble as teen-agers. Her family was horrified when she put her children on the bus and sent them anywhere in the city. Sometimes they would travel alone all the way to Maywood to stay with their grandparents or their aunt. But that was the only way they would learn: they should not be too sheltered. She wanted Daniel, above all, to be responsible and independent.

She often sent Daniel, who was ten years old, on errands. He and Carla knew how to dry clothes at the laundromat: Harriet gave him the money and he knew where to go and how to operate the machines. At home, both children answered the phone for Harriet and were taught how to take messages when she was not there. Once when Harriet ordered new linoleum, she had Daniel stay home from school to receive the delivery.

Daniel took good care of Carla and always protected her. He once got into a fight with a boy who put a water pistol in her face. Now, however, Carla was learning to defend herself.

Harriet did not want to inhibit her children or to prevent them from growing up. When six-year-old Carla said she liked a boy who was much older than herself, Harriet's only comment was that she should find one her own age. She took her children everywhere: to plays, to museums, to the park. She could remember being taken somewhere only once by her own parents, and that was to Brookfield Zoo. Often, Daniel came to Harriet's place of work, bringing Carla, and she took them somewhere after work—to the zoo, shopping, or to their grandparents' house.

Harriet did not trust the world; when it came to her children, she trusted herself only. She was determined, however, not to lock them away from the world as her parents had done to her, but rather to direct them away from its dangers and

toward those things of which she approved. She wanted to assure them of a pleasant and active, yet disciplined, life. She tried to protect them from their environment by teaching them to be dependent on one another and aloof from everyone
and everything she disliked or feared.

Arnold, Lucille Foster's son, was far less self-sufficient than Harriet's Daniel and
had fewer responsibilities. Born rather late in Lucille's life and under special circumstances, he was his Mama's "love child." Because he was a winsome, happy child,
it was easy to give him the special place in his mother's heart that every child
craves. He ran to meet her after work and hugged and kissed her, really making
her feel wanted. When he was nine, however, she noticed signs of his becoming
"mannish." His behavior toward her, became a bit more reserved, at least in public.
One day he came home and complained about his "dumb math teacher"; she had
told Arnold that his mother "must feed him with a spoon". Somewhat worried,
Arnold asked his mother if she pampered him. She said that she did not. At about
the same time, Arnold complained about the elderly gentleman, whom Lucille had
hired to walk the boys home from school, staying with them until she got home.
Arnold felt that he was too old for that. Lucille agreed and decided to let the boys
fend for themselves until she got home at 4:30.

Arnold knew his father and saw him frequently, but he could not really depend
on him from day to day. He was always ready to go anywhere with an adult, and
was not above soliciting money or special favors from them when he could; his
mother managed to keep some check on this, however, and scolded him for it.
Sylvester gave Arnold money and sometimes brought his sons over to play with him.
Arnold made the best of whatever came his way in the form of attention and
entertainment, although much of the time he was lonely.

In his preschool years and later on in the summers, Arnold stayed with friends
of Lucille's, women who had to stay home with small children or an invalid husband.
As he grew older, Arnold dreaded this, preferring to stay home and play with his
friends and counting on the occasional concern of adults to help vary his routine.
But when Robert, his older brother, got a job and began to work after school,
Arnold was increasingly left alone. Lucille worried about this, trying to make up for
it by spending more time with him.

It was not only his father that Arnold missed: he felt cut off from his "brothers
and sisters"—his father's other family. He grew quite excited when he was anywhere in the vicinity of their home, and he was overjoyed whenever his father took
him to see them. He felt somewhat the same about Sylvester's boys. And when I
took Arnold to visit Harriet's children, Daniel and Carla, one day, all three children
were pleased. Although Lucille and Harriet had known each other for years, they
had never visited with their children.

On that occasion, it was first established that Daniel was only a few months
older than Arnold, not old enough to be really threatening; then they settled down
to play together. Daniel had every kind of toy imaginable, expensive and inexpen-
sive, and Arnold was excited. His mother bought him few toys, because she was
trying to save money. Harriet's view was that the future would take care of itself.

When it was time to leave, Harriet told Daniel to see Arnold to the car; he said
he could not, because his hands were full (he had a toy gun in each hand). But after

we got out to the car, Daniel came running out the back way with a toy rifle, which he handed to Arnold. He asked me if I would bring the gun back when I came the next day. Suspecting a plan of some kind, I agreed. The next day, Arnold called me and announced that he "could go" to Daniel's that day. The urgency with which this little drama was enacted highlighted the needs and loneliness of the children.

Arnold really wanted a brother his own age; he didn't get along well with his older brother, Robert. While Lucille and Sylvester were breaking up, the two boys fought constantly, nearly driving Lucille "out of her mind." Robert did not want Sylvester in his home, while Arnold looked to him as a potential father.

Becoming a Man in a Matrifocal Household: Robert   Robert was not as friendly and outgoing as Arnold. Robert, Sr. was a quiet man, in contrast to Lewison, Arnold's father, who was sociable nearly to the point of being effusive. As far as anyone knew, Robert was his father's only child, although he did not really take much interest in his son. His problems with Lucille had kept him from thinking much about Robert, Jr.

When Robert was born, his father's parents were very proud of him. He was black, like a Foster, even as a baby; Lucille had never seen a baby like that; usually they were sort of pink. His father said, "If he's not mine, at least he must be a Foster."

Robert Foster had taken his son South to see his grandparents twice. The first time he had left him there and gone on somewhere else, although he had promised Lucille to bring him back. He told his parents that he had given Lucille the fare to come and get Robert, but that was a lie, she insisted. He had not given her a cent. So Robert had stayed there all summer, which was what his father wanted.

When Robert was older, his father took both him and Arnold to his parents' farm, where they stayed for the summer. That year for the first time Lucille went on a vacation; she flew to Detroit and then to Canada. But Robert later reported that his grandmother had "been mean" to Arnold, so Lucille regretted that summer. When Robert was sixteen, his father again decided to take him South, but Lucille would not let him go. She did not like the way Robert, Sr. had planned the trip, because he discussed it with Robert first and then "announced" to Lucile that they were going. She was angry at both of them and criticized her son and husband severely. The boy merely sat there, hurt and withdrawn.

Robert resented Lucille's favoritism toward Arnold as he grew older. He was in the shadow of his younger brother's appealing personality and retreated even more, although he was very observant. He began to write poetry and essays—beautiful, imaginative, but strange, compositions, which revealed deep sensitivity and suffering. His teachers encouraged him in his writing and recommended him for a scholarship to college.

In his senior year, Robert began to grow more independent of Lucille. He got a job and had spending money, although Lucille tried to control his spending to some extent. He had a girlfriend, Suzy, who lived in Evanston with her mother and whose stepfather lived upstairs from the Fosters'. She and Robert got together when Suzy visited her stepfather; at other times, he talked to her on the phone for hours, looking relaxed and happy. Once or twice, Lucille took Arnold and Robert to

Evanston to visit Suzy and her mother. At Suzy's request, her mother was thinking about letting her stay with her stepfather in Chicago during the summer. But Lucille was against this, fearing that she would become a grandmother at too young an age. Suzy did not come that summer.

Robert was in awe of his mother's firm authority and her temper, but he began to speak up more, possibly encouraged by his father. Although he disliked Sylvester, he felt a basic sympathy with him, especially when his mother "got on Sylvester's case." Once he drew a cartoon showing Sylvester in a doghouse with the caption "Come on out." Overhead was a cloud labeled "Sex hate" and "Lucille." No one knew what went on in Robert's mind: least of all Lucille.

When he was not at school or working, Robert spent most of his time at home. He began to go to "Operation Breadbasket" every Saturday morning, and the young Reverend Jesse Jackson, the heir apparent to Martin Luther King, became one of his heroes. "Operation Breadbasket" was a new-style revival meeting, with music and sermonizing for all ages. Reverend Jackson himself—"the country preacher," in leather vest and sideburns—was appealing to both young and old; his messages were a mixture of old time religion, militancy, and economic realism. Dedicated but "hip," Jesse Jackson was a strong attraction for a young Black man trying to find himself. "I am Somebody!" was Jackson's message, and Robert responded wholeheartedly.

Robert's other idol was Eldridge Cleaver, whose books he devoured. He let his hair grow into an "Afro" and bought a dashiki, over Lucille's protests. He also talked about joining the Black Panther Party. Lucille who had for years been keeping him out of the Blackstone Rangers, was angered. She warned him that if he got into trouble, he would have to find his own way out. He could not expect any help from her. She distrusted the new trend toward militancy, with its overtones of male dominance; she felt it boded ill for families.

Once Robert threatened to move out and Lucille told him to go ahead, although she privately said she did not think he would. If he went to live with his father, it would be too far from school, and he could not afford to rent a room. Lucille's sister criticized her for her treatment of Robert, telling her that she would be sorry some day for it. Robert, Sr. called and said he had heard that she was kicking his son out. Lucille answered, "Sure, do you want him?" But Robert stayed with his mother.

When Robert graduated from high school, his father bought him an Edwardian suit with a blue shirt and matching tie. He looked dashing on the night of the prom: he was a tall young man and his "natural" was becoming to his rather full face. Lucille took many pictures of him and Suzy before they left for the dance.

Lucille had struggled to pay Robert's tuition through all the years with little help from his father, and now she did not regret it. He was planning to go on to college; he was safe, whole, and assured of a future. She had not provided her children with one father, but she had made sure that they were looked after and were made the concern of the men in her life. Soon both of them would be grown, she reflected, and she needed to start thinking of herself.

Most ethnographers of Black communities have been men; as a result, many interpretations of Black male and female roles reflect a male bias. An instance of

Graduation day

what I believe to be a false issue partly arising from such a bias is that of the problem of masculine identification in a matrifocal household. It should be noted that in few societies has the role of mother been as undermined and generally held suspect as in middle-class, upwardly mobile America, where a strong mother is open to accusations of "Momism." In Pakistani and Indian families, mothers are strongly protective, nurturant, and held in great respect, as in many family-oriented cultures. While the mother yields the final authority to a man in these societies, she has much power and influence over her children. Further, while her husband has authority over her, he is under the authority of his father, mother, and elder brother, so that a boy does not look to his father as an absolute authority; rather, he learns early about the realistic limitations and relativity of power in social relationships within his family.

No particular family structure can be deemed necessary to raise children successfully, nor is any type of family a guarantee of success. A boy can learn how to exercise his rights and authority from any model, male or female. On the other hand, an over-dominated child is equally oppressed whether the source of that oppression is male or female. The real problem in Black communities is not that of female domination *per se*, but that of the single-parent household, where one adult, usually the mother, must bear the burden of socialization, even support, by herself; this may put severe strains on her relationship with her children. As we have seen, in the Black family this is often mitigated by the help of grandparents, godparents, aunts, uncles, sisters, and brothers, even neighbors, in raising her children; and male members of her family, as well as the men in her life, serve as role models to her young son.

As pointed out by Hannerz and others (1969),[1] furthermore, a mother treats her son differently than her daughter, consciously socializing him to a male role. A

[1] Ulf, Hannerz, *Soulside: Inquiries into Ghetto Culture and Community.* New York: Columbia University Press, 1969.

son may rebel against the role type that his mother tries to impose on him; however, he finds many alternatives within his extended family, among family friends, in churches and other institutions, and on the streets. Although his mother may claim to be a definitive source of what it means to be a man, he soon learns to look to a real source, to a man in his mother's life who may be a living contradiction of her views—as husband or lover, father, older son, or brother. The young Black man raised by his mother may thus actually be fortunate in having a choice of role types, rather than having one thrust upon him to imitate or rebel against; he is more free to choose his own way of being a man. And while he may feel resentment toward a dominant mother, he also feels love and respect for a harried, hardworking mentor who has given him the safety and security she could provide.

PEOPLE NEED PEOPLE

Security in Extended Families   Perhaps the most effective way of protecting young people from the hazards of city life is by surrounding them with a wide circle of family and friends. Children play with cousins and other relatives; family members and friends take turns watching each other's children, and as children grow up, much time that would otherwise be spent on the streets is spent with relatives. Children learn about life through adults around them to whom they are close; they do not have to experience everything themselves to know what life in the ghetto is like.

On Chicago's West Side, in one of the city's roughest sections, Angela Martin lives with her family. They live on the top floor of a three-story building, in a nicely kept and well-furnished apartment shared by Angela and her son, her mother, stepfather and two small sisters, and her Cousin Rona with her two children.

Rona is the daughter of Angela's mother's youngest sister; her mother died several years ago, leaving four children, two boys and two girls. The two girls came to live with their aunt and the boys remained with their father; later, when their father was having difficulties handling things by himself, Rona's sister went back home to help him out. Rona, who is twenty, has two children and babysits while Angela and her mother work. She would like to work, also, but neither of the other two wants to give up her job. Angela has worked at her company for two years and is on a profit-sharing plan; her mother is a beautician and her stepfather is a medical technician.

Angela's mother has ten brothers and sisters, most of whom live in Chicago. Her family moved from Mississippi when she was five and settled on the West Side; as they grew up, one brother moved to Gary, Indiana and another to the South Side, but most of them remained on the West Side. Two of her sisters have died in the past few years, and both times they held large funerals which were attended by great numbers of kinfolk, including those had remained in the South. They all stayed with their relatives on the West Side. The Southern kin also came to a distant cousin's wedding last year, although they did not stay as long.

Angela sees her maternal relatives quite often, although she has one girlfriend her age who is closer in some ways than her cousins. Besides Cousin Rona, she sees most frequently some distant "cousins" whose mother, Persia, is said to be related to Angela's grandmother. Angela doubledates with her cousins and met her son's father through them. Persia has moved further West, out of the immediate neighborhood, but her mother lives in the same building as some of her grandchildren and great-grandchildren, and she sometimes babysits for them in the evenings.

Although Angela's mother and father have been separated for seventeen years, she still sees her father twice a week and has kept in close touch with his side of the family. Her stepfather is more like an older brother than a father to Angela. A young-looking man, he used to live in Hyde Park and recalls with nostalgia the swinging night life that characterized that neighborhood in the old days. Angela has not gotten to know his family well, probably because she has kept in close touch with her own father and his family.

Angela is a light-hearted young girl who likes to go out at night, as do her relatives. They are a lively bunch, and nicknames abound: Aunt "Angel," Uncle "Sugar," Aunt "Pie" are just a few of them. Persia and her daughters were present at the recent opening of "Sam and the Twins," a tavern on the West Side owned by a pair of twins and their cousin, old friends of Angela's family. Many of the old family friends who had moved away from the West Side were there. Angela enjoyed the opening, and she spent many subsequent evenings at "Sam and the Twins," even "spinning disks" for the "DJ" sometimes when he wanted a break. Although Angela feels she met a "wrong dude" in the father of her son, she has remained a fairly well protected young woman among her family and friends.

Lois: A Family and a "Stepfamily"   Lois McCoy has had serious difficulties early in her life; nevertheless, she has carried on with finishing school and planning for her own as well as her son's future. She lives in one of the worst neighborhoods in Chicago, surrounded by poverty, misery, and crime. But aside from her troubles with Dean, Lois, too, has lived a sheltered life within her family group.

Lois's mother's relatives live on the South Side, in addition to most of her stepfather's relatives; both families are close-knit, and Lois sees her aunts, uncles, and cousins often. She grew up with her cousins, and she is still closer to them than to anyone else with the exception of one friend, a neighbor, who introduced her to Dean.

Lois has three sets of grandparents: her mother's parents, her real father's parents, and her stepfather's parents. She remembers her mother's father and mother well; they are both dead now. They came over to visit every week when they were living. Her real father's parents live in Kansas City and she sees them about twice a year. They come every year on their vacation and always come for funerals. Her stepfather's parents—"Grandaddy" and "Grandmom" Taylor—come up from St. Louis three times every year. Of course, all the family gets together when the older people come for a visit. Lois even recalls her grandmother's brother and his wife, who used to live nearby; she pierced Lois's ears when she was just a child. Lois remembers attending both of their funerals.

Besides her grandparents, Lois does not know any of her real father's family, but she has adopted her stepfather's relatives as her own. Two of her stepfather's sisters live in St. Louis, and she and her stepfather go down every year for her Aunt Marie's birthday. Aunt Marie had a barbecue in her backyard one year on her birthday, and Lois, her two younger sisters, and some of her cousins went. They all gave Aunt Marie a birthday gift; then, according to custom, they gave her money when they left. Lois and her sisters each gave her 10 dollars.

Two of the other St. Louis aunt's children died when they were in their twenties: a girl, who was a nurse, died of pneumonia, and a boy was killed by the police in a narcotics arrest. Lois was present at both funerals, which were less than a year apart; she stayed one or two weeks each time. Her stepfather also went to his nephew's funeral. Lois was surprised to note that the mourners all wore white instead of black; the men wore black crepe armbands. They belonged to a religious sect that she had never heard of in Chicago.

One of the cousins on Lois's stepfather's side, Warrington, who lives in Chicago, sends his Aunt Marie and her sister round-trip tickets to Chicago every year, and then arranges a reunion of the Chicago relatives. His own mother is dead. Two of his cousins, who live in Chicago, also lost their mother and were raised by Aunt Marie. They had married two brothers, but both left their husbands and moved to Chicago, staying together with their children. Warrington makes certain that they are included in family gatherings. He tries to keep the St. Louis and Chicago branches of the family in touch, and he visits Lois's family nearly every day and the other cousins almost as often. While he is not particularly wealthy or influential, he plays a crucial role in keeping his family together.

Lois's mother's family has fewer reunions and formal get-togethers, because they all live close to one another and see each other often; Lois's mother recently gave a party on her sister's birthday and they had a going-away party when a cousin went into the service. They used to have picnics on holidays, too. Once they went out to Forest Preserve for a picnic on Memorial Day. Someone laughed about that to Lois, saying, "Most families decorate graves on Memorial Day, but you went on a picnic?" Lois did not think it was particularly funny; that's just what they had decided to do.

Lois's mother's family had moved to Chicago when she was about eleven. She still remembers a lot of things about life down South. She feels that her own children's life is a lot easier than hers was and that they are spoiled. All of her brothers and sisters had big families; one sister died at a young age, leaving a large brood of young children to be cared for. Since the aunts and uncles could not take the children, they were put in foster homes. Lois sees these cousins often, especially the boys, who drive by several times a week. They go to Dunbar High, where some of Lois's other cousins also attend school.

When Lois's older sister, Marilyn, died, another married sister who had no children took hers. She had taken care of them once before, when Marilyn had disappeared for almost a year. She sent them back to Marilyn when she returned, saying, "After all, she's my sister; if she wants her children, she should have them." Marilyn always said to them: "If anything happens to me, I know Laura will take care of you." She seemed to feel that something would happen. Later she died of a brain hemorrhage. Lois reported:

> She fell while putting up curtains: I guess that caused it. She didn't tell (the doctors) that, though, and they only told her she had high blood pressure when she went to see them about her headaches.

She was over here Christmas Eve. She lay down and slept all day. My little sister told my mother, "She's been sleeping all day and her feet are so cold." My mother went in and woke her up and asked if she felt all right. All she would say was, "Uhuh, Uhuh, Uhuh," so Mama said, "She must be in a coma," and we took her to the hospital. She never came out of it.

Lois had just begun to get close to her sister when she died. "She was so hard to talk to. Maybe she wanted to die." Lois's mother had the children for awhile after her daughter died, but she had too many young children of her own. Laura was happy to take them.

In Lois's family, "belongingness" to a large family group and the observance of obligations of many kinds to relatives develops in children a strong social sense. This is evident in later life as sisters and aunts take over the task of raising younger family members when a death in the family deprives them of a mother, and as all members take responsibility for a fatherless child, or for any children who need help. The general willingness to take in any relatives reflects and in turn strengthens family bonds, as does the observance of family rituals—funerals, birthdays, reunions—which establishes the continuity of the family and the importance of its members.

Lois and Adrienne: Grandparents, "Play-Relatives," and Kindly Neighbors
Besides her relatives by birth and by marriage, Lois had a "godmother," as she refers to her. Lois has not heard the term "play-mother," but her godmother was more like a "play-mother" than a real godmother. When she was fourteen, Lois was standing on the street one day when the ice cream man came by. She had spent her money and could not buy ice cream; a lady across the street called her over and asked why she did not. Lois explained that she had spent all her money, so the woman bought ice cream for her.

Lois's godmother asked her over to visit, and one time she asked if her mother

Getting acquainted

would mind if she bought her a coat. Lois said she did not think she would mind. Her godmother also bought Lois a present on her birthday.

When Deanie was born, the woman wanted to buy things for him, too, but when Lois told Dean, Sr., he objected: "Maybe she could buy you, but not him." So Lois stopped seeing her "godmother." When she saw her once afterward, her godmother said, "I guess I'll have to get me a new godchild."

Adrienne Vincent has never heard the term "play-mother," either, although when she was younger she called a neighbor "Mama" and spent weekends with her. She says she was like a grandmother to her, because she did not have a grandmother living. Now her "play-grandmother" lives in the next apartment with her own daughter, who is married to Adrienne's uncle.

A grandmother is important to a child. Adrienne's little sister, Jeanette, misses having a grandmother, too; she calls the grandmother of the little girls across the walk "Grandma." They exchange gifts; Adrienne's mother gives her a gift at Christmas and her "play-grandmother" gives Jeanette gifts at Christmas, on her birthday, and at other times. "Play-relatives" give these children a sense of a familiar, supportive world beyond their family.

Adrienne's maternal grandmother died when she was small; she only saw her once, when they visited her in St. Louis. Her paternal grandmother died when her father was young; her father's father, who deserted his family before his wife died, suddenly reappeared in Chicago a number of years ago and Adrienne's mother persuaded her husband to let him stay with them, although at first he did not like the idea; he was still angry at him for leaving his family. Her family had always been close, but her husband had lost track of his. His older brother had left home years before because he was in trouble with the police; Adrienne herself had seen him once or twice. The old man, Adrienne's grandfather, had stayed with her parents for awhile, then disappeared again. He ultimately turned up and stayed with Aunt Lorraine until his death a few years later. Though in short supply, old people are provided for in Adrienne's family as well as the young.

Learning Adult Roles   Because Adrienne's father lost his parents while he was young, he feels strongly about giving children parental care and guidance. He does not think that a mother should work; Adrienne's mother stayed home with her three oldest children until Adrienne, the youngest, was twelve; then she hired a woman to come in and stay with them while she worked at the tavern. She jokingly told Adrienne that she could not stand being home with them any longer, because they were so bad. Now she stays home with Jeanette, who is five.

In this tightly-knit, hard-working family, children take on strong personalities while young. Jeanette, Adrienne's youngest sister, acts quite adult for her age, and so does her niece—her oldest sister's daughter, Jan—who is about the same age. Jan's mother, who was separated for awhile from her husband, works, and "Grandma" takes care of Jan. Adrienne and her mother and sister share many anecdotes about Jeanette and Jan and their odd, adultlike behavior, which no doubt encourages their eccentricities. Jeanette has recently learned to dial the phone and called her sister five or six times on that first day; she still calls almost every day:

Yesterday she called and said, "Hello, Adrienne, have you taken care of your children today? Have you cleaned your house? Have you gotten dinner for your husband? That's good: I just called to see if you were taking care of business." She (Jeanette) calls me "Adrienne"; sometimes she calls me "darling." She's so dramatic about everything; she'll say, "Oh, darling, I'm glad you came," then laugh and run away. She calls everyone "darling," I guess because my father calls her that.

In "acting out" roles, Jeanette is both playing and at the same time "trying on" social alternatives. When she plays with Adrienne's daughter, Caroline, age three, she lets her know that she is her superior: "Now I'm your aunt . . . you have to do whatever I say." She dresses herself carefully; she has a closetful of clothes, and her parents give her everything she wants. Once, though, she came over to Adrienne's house wearing a flowered blouse and plaid pants. Adrienne reported:

> When we told her that, she said, "That's not all! I have on two pairs of panties." I asked why, and she said "Because I'm going to stay overnight: one for today, one for tomorrow."

Adrienne and her mother and sister call Jeanette and Jan "little old ladies"; the teachers at school call Jan "old maid" because she is very articulate and "bossy." According to Adrienne:

> She's the most honest kid I've ever known. If she thinks something, she'll say it out. She doesn't mean anything by it. Once she was over here and Roger's stepfather came by; Roger was upstairs at her mother's so I asked her to go call him. She said, "Roger's stepfather? If he has a step*father* where's his step-*mother?*" She sounded real smart, but she didn't mean anything; it was just what she was thinking about.

Children in Adrienne's family think about social roles and learn adult attitudes and values at an early age. Jeanette attempts to relate as a peer to her older sisters; both Jeanette and Jan play adult roles *vis-à-vis* Caroline, who is three. Striving to compete with her Aunt Jeanette, Jan also adopts a "mature" air. While her father was separated from her mother, he called and Jan answered the phone, saying to him, "You don't want to talk to me, noway: you want to talk to my

"Sisters"

mother" and handed the phone to her mother. On another occasion she came over to Adrienne's house when Adrienne's mother was visiting and asked to borrow her cousin Caroline's "trike." Adrienne's mother told her that they were leaving and could not get it down. So she left, remarking as she closed the door, "I'm going, and I'm walking 'cause you won't do nothin' for me."

Adrienne's daughter, Caroline, also on occasion "acts out" adult roles. She requested that her grandmother give her a car for Christmas and her grandmother asked her, "One you can pedal?' Caroline, three, answered, "No, one you can drive." Another time when the children were with Adrienne's mother they bought some hot dogs and took them home; when her father complained that they did not bring him any, Jeanette replied, "If you'd stay home sometime, you'd get some."

These children were becoming adept at the verbal repartee that is characteristic in Black communities, while anticipating an adult social identity; the constant commentary on the part of their elders concerning the children's behavior encourages their early development. But as with adults, "things" sometimes "got to" children. When Jeanette was three, she used to run away from home often:

> She'd leave early in the morning, six o'clock. When my mother got up at seven, she'd be gone. She took the dog with her. We'd really get scared and go looking for her. We'd find her walking down the street with the dog, blocks away. I was trying to think how mother stopped her . . . oh, she put a lock on the fence.

A Family Symbol   Humorous stories about family members are important in Adrienne's family, as in many others; they help to establish family and individual identity. The family "folktales" about the dog, King, who has been a staunch member and supporter of the family for many years, communicate much of the flavor of family life and its perceptions:

> The dog's gone now: he didn't come back this time; he's been gone about two weeks. My mother said she's glad, since he's been running away a lot and every-time it costs her money. One time he came back with a cut paw and she had to take him to the vet; it cost fifteen dollars. Then another time his eye was slit down the side and he had to have stitches. Then he ran away again and got his stitches opened up; that time, the vet had to keep him for a week. This time my mother said, "If he shows his face this time, I'll just tell him, "Stay on out there if you like it so well:" But he hasn't come back; he must have got run over or hurt too bad. He would come back if he could move at all. He's not a friendly dog, so probably no one would take him. He'd like some people but others he couldn't stand. Like the laundry man: he didn't like him at all. I don't know what that man had done to him; he said he hadn't done anything, but some neighbors said they saw him teasing the dog one time. One time he came and the dog was out. My mother said, "Come on in until we find the dog." He said, "Oh, the dog's out?" and came into the kitchen fast. In the meantime, I went out and found King standing by the man's truck: he was waiting for him. So I took him upstairs and told the man, "He was waiting for you: I don't know what you've done to my dog." He hated that man so much he used to tear up the bags he brought the laundry in. And he'd tear the plastic covers off the clean clothes when he knew we weren't looking and start shaking his head, tearing them up. My mother would say, "Fool, what do you think you're doing?"

Separation in Adrienne's family actually involved little physical distance and the maintenance of a high degree of social and economic interchange; still, the establishment of new "families of procreation" meant the disruption of the deep solidarity growing out of continuous daily contact. The family watchdog—a symbol of the safety and protection arising from such solidarity—also left home; and now a puppy with enormous ears and paws was chewing up slippers and, Adrienne complained, was being a general nuisance in her household.

The family legends and stories about pets, children, and other family members were commentaries on life and on humankind; everything truly important, they seemed to imply, happens within an intimate circle. Children were learning to influence and in turn be directed and influenced by those who were essential to their well-being; they might desire to escape the rigorous restraints of family life temporarily; but their orientation, the meaning of their existence lay, ultimately, within the family.

LEARNING THE RULES

Authority, Discipline, and Benevolence Childhood in Black communities involves a continuous flirtation with the forbidden, a frequent drawing and testing of boundaries, a repeated assertion and challenging of authority, in short, a constant crossing of wills. The respect for authority and for the home, responsibility for oneself and for others, honesty (but not to the point of foolishness), and skills necessary to survive in an unfavorable environment must be imparted in an atmosphere which is often subversive of those very values. Therefore, the sense of territory is developed at an early age, as mothers try to keep their children close to home. For young children and, later on, for girls, this is not a great problem, but as boys grow up, they tend to wander away to find their own domains.

When Adrienne was a child her parents had a big yard; she never liked to play in it, so she went across the street to her friend's house instead. They did not even have a yard; she sat on the porch. She noticed that her own children and the others in the building never played in the yard, either, but stayed on the porch most of the time. They went on occasional forays into other parts of the neighborhood for purposes of mischief. When that happened, one of the children usually informed her and she was right after them.

None of the children in the neighborhood went to the park, although it was only two blocks away. They played ball in the street where they could break someone's window. It was probably because their mothers liked to have them close by, Adrienne observed.

Adrienne had never gone to the park either as a child, although it had been right across the street. She played elsewhere in the neighborhood—in her friends' yards and homes—but she and her brother had to be home by dark. She always made it in time, but her brother, Thomas, never could. Even in the summer, when daylight remained longer, he could not get home by dark. He got into trouble everytime, but it did not make any difference. His mother told him, "All right, but if you get caught over curfew, don't call me to get you."

He kept staying out until he finally did get caught; when he called his mother, she refused to go get him that night. She said, "I'll come tomorrow." He protested, "Tomorrow! I don't want to stay here tonight!" She told him, "Then you shouldn't have been out there." After that, he came home at the proper time.

Adrienne and Thomas were "bad" a lot; they fought all the time and always did things they should not have done. Their older sister was different. She never did anything wrong. She always said, "But mother said . . ." and they replied, "Who cares what mother said?" and went right ahead with their plans. But she never squealed on them. She never got punished, except when she would not "tell on" her brother and sister. Adrienne's mother punished everyone for this offense. She was petite and weighed only 103 pounds, but she was strong. She did not like it if one of them smiled when she hit the others, and she promptly hit him, too.

Adrienne and her brother were sometimes punished for a week or two. Once they were playing on their mother's chair, when they broke one of the back legs, which could not be seen. They propped it up with bricks. Their mother was working at the time and had a woman come in to do the cleaning, so she did not discover it until she quit work. Then they had to stay in their rooms for two weeks. She took away their radio, as well as anything else for entertainment.

When Adrienne's brother did not come home from school on time, his mother went after him and whipped him all the way home. He was with his friends and was highly embarrassed, but his mother was unaffected by his protests.

They rode their bikes at three or four o'clock in the morning. They had a good thing going, and their friends slipped out and joined them. It was because of Adrienne that they were finally discovered. She did tricks on her bike, and they all dared her to stand on the seat. She tried this feat and hit a tree; her bike went one way and she went the other. She began to scream and their parents heard her. They came out, and after she bandaged Adrienne's skinned knees, their mother gave both of them a whipping.

The next battleground was smoking. Thomas learned first, then he taught Adrienne. When their mother caught them, she made them eat the cigarettes. But this did not stop Adrienne from smoking. Her mother came into her room unexpectedly, and Adrienne hid her cigarette under the bed. Before she left, her mother said, "Please take that cigarette up before you start a fire." Finally, Adrienne asked her for permission to smoke. She said, "All right, but always buy your own cigarettes; don't accept them from anyone else." So that's what Adrienne did; she only borrowed them from her mother or her sister:

> But my mother is really something; she'll get ready to go home and say, "Where are my cigarettes?" She probably has smoked them, but I'll give her mine and say, "Here are some, probably mine." She'll say, "Not yours, mine: I brought a pack here." So I won't argue with her.

Adrienne's mother punished them severely for lying. Once her brother did not come home when he should have and his mother asked him where he had been. He said, "At Aunt Lorraine's." However, she had called there and knew he wasn't there. She just hit him hard, without saying a word. Adrienne smiled and she asked her what she was smiling at. Adrienne replied, "Oh, it's a nice day," and she threatened, "Oh, you want it for lying?" Then Adrienne had to admit that she had smiled because her mother had hit her brother.

Adrienne's mother hated lies so much that she would not tell her children any. They never believed in Santa Claus. But she gave Adrienne a beating when she told the neighbor's children that there was no Santa Claus. The mothers complained that their kids were talking about it and getting upset; she told Adrienne not to say those things. She had to learn when honesty meant unkindness.

Adrienne's father was not a strict disciplinarian:

> My father talks in his sleep all the time, usually about work; he'll be talking to customers. My mother only says one word in her sleep, and that's, "No." My father will never say "No," only "Yes." He used to bring things home; one time he brought a big box of those candy turtles. Someone who was in business brought them to the tavern: he was always getting things like that. We ate and ate those turtles. My father told us we couldn' have anymore. Then, when he was asleep, we asked him if we could have some and he said, "Yes." When he woke up he saw us eating them and said, "Who told you you could have those?" We said, "You did."

When Adrienne was eleven and her brother was thirteen, they stole their father's car and went for joyrides. Their father came home at night and slept for awhile, then picked up their mother at closing time. While he was asleep, they took the keys out of his pocket and went for a ride. He found out about it when someone had taken his parking place when they returned the car, and they had to park it in a different place. But he did not do too much about it. By that time, Thomas was almost sixteen, and he got him a driving permit.

Adrienne did not resent her mother for punishing them.

> We would have been worse if she hadn't punished us. One time when my brother was bigger, he thought he didn't have to do what she said; he raised his hand to hit her and she gave him a backhand that knocked him across the floor and he hit his head on the refrigerator. He was knocked out for several minutes. She's strong for a little woman.

Adrienne thought her younger sister would really be bad; her mother is much easier on her than she was with them. She is the only one at home now, so she is spoiled. Her father disciplines her, but he buys her everything she wants: she has three radios, a record player, TV, two bicycles—a large one for later on and a three-wheeler. She has two rooms (one is a play room), and she has more clothes than Adrienne and her sister and daughter combined. She is very clothes conscious: she would not eat ice cream because she was afraid she might get it on her dress. She is very polite and the teachers in school like her. She is not "bad" like Adrienne and her brother were; she also does not have a mischievous brother her age to give her ideas.

Adrienne is not a strong disciplinarian with her daughter and son. She uses persuasion with Caroline, verbally and through her actions. As a punishment, she sends her to bed early or else does not allow her to watch TV. When Caroline was going to run away from home because she felt that her mother did not like her, Adrienne said, "OK, but put on your coat: it's cold." Caroline got out the door, then came back in. Adrienne asked, "What's the matter? I thought you were going." Caroline replied, "No, it's too cold."

Caroline plays every day with Adrienne's brother's little boy, who is younger than she is:

That little boy is a mean one; he bites. He bit her arm one time so hard the blood came. But she won't hit him or bite him back. I used to try to stop one of them when they did something to the other; then the other would say, "Oh, he didn't mean it." So one time when Caroline came downstairs crying because he hit her, I said, "Oh, he didn't mean it."

Adrienne does not understand her little boy, who seldom cries, not even when he falls down; if she hits him, he just laughs at her. Her mother says it is because he is a boy, but she does not agree. He listens to his father, who is even a sterner disciplinarian than Adrienne's mother. Adrienne's brother, too, is very strict.

Although all parents agree on the need for discipline, its method and frequency is seen to be partly a matter of personality and temperament. Likewise, the same technique will affect one child one way, another differently, since they are individuals in their own right. No handbook for raising children exists, but only the dictates of wisdom and good sense—of which everyone has his own ideas.

Imparting Values: Lucille   Lucille Foster was strict with her boys, especially with the oldest, Robert. She resented his plays for independence; she did not appreciate his admiration for the Black Panthers, his Afro hairstyle, and the dashiki. Now that he had a job and some money of his own, he felt pretty independent, almost like he could do whatever he wanted. He came home late from school one evening and she demanded an explanation. She told him he was "crazy" if he thought he could just do what he wanted to. He said, "*I'm* not crazy: *you're* the one that's crazy"; "You say I'm crazy and I'm supporting you . . ." she declared, and when he persisted, repeating "You're crazy," she took after him with a mop and broke the handle on him.

After that episode, Lucille threatened to make him leave. But Robert stayed.

Although Lucille hated his sullen, whining ways around the house, she was secretly proud of her big, rather brilliant son. She kept all his school essays and occasionally read them to friends. She said she did not know what his plans were: whether or where he planned to go to college. He never told her anything. But she knew that he was going on to school: that was the only way "up" for a young man. She had not paid all that tuition for nothing!

Lucille did not mind some of Robert's "secrets" as much as she did others. When Arnold found an empty Ripple bottle in the room they shared, she said little. He said, "Aren't you going to say anything to him about it?" but she only replied, "If Robert knows you told on him, he'd hit you upside the head!" Usually she approved of "telling"; but this was Robert's own business. Again, when she found a book about sex among teenagers in Robert's drawer, she read it and laughed about it to her friends. When it came to money, Lucille tolerated no secrets.

Lucille was in no way greedy or stingy, but money was sacred to her. It had been scarce throughout most of her life; now she always managed to put a little away for contingencies. She worked hard and was able to buy the necessities for her sons and herself, but whenever any of her men friends had some extra money her instincts led her to it like a divining rod to water. When work was slack, it paid some of the bills, and at other times it paid for a new outfit or something for the house. No man could get money from her: when Lewison tried it, he was quickly straightened out on the matter. She always put her children first, and later on, when they were older, she began to think of herself.

When Robert began to work Lucille borrowed money from him now and then, when she was low on funds. She was on private duty, and sometimes her patients were late in paying her. She asked to see Robert's bankbook and he told her he had lost it; he said he had lost some money too. When she asked him again, he said he had sent the book in to the bank and had not gotten it back. Lucille was angry; she knew he was lying and trying to hide something from her. If there was anything she hated, it was a lie. She refused to take him to football practice in Forest Preserve that week and said he could not go to Operation Breadbasket. When he said he wanted to spend the money on a Christmas present for his girlfriend, she said to me:

He better not spend a lot of money on Suzy . . . Christmas around here is not going to be very happy, I can tell you . . . I'm not going to work my tail off to do things for the kids when they don't appreciate it.

Yet when Christmas came, Lucille bought Robert an expensive set of matching knit pants and sweater, and he bought her an electric mixer.

Life Is a Gamble: Harriet   Harriet had a different view of money than her friend; briefly, it could be summarized as "easy come, easy go." Money had not been particularly scarce in her home, since both parents had worked. When she was on her own, she had boundless confidence that it would come from somewhere, and usually, it did. She wrote out checks with no money in the bank to cover them; she knew that eventually there would be money there. When she had a baby in her early thirties, she went on welfare and continued to work at two or three jobs. The authorities caught up with her and threatened to put her in jail. She said, "If you can find someone to take care of my children, all right," but they never did a thing to her.

Like Lucille, Harriet accepted money from men friends, but she gave it to someone for whom she cared. After her bitter experience with a younger man, she contented herself with giving gifts and with generous hospitality to her friends.

Harriet's rather cavalier attitude toward money could also be seen in other members of her family. When Harriet and I visited her Cousin Reba, money became a topic of conversation when Reba's daughter lost a twenty dollar bill; she had folded it up and dropped it on the floor, where she later found it. She then casually dropped it down her front, saying she was always losing money like that.

Her daughter's carelessness led to a discourse on Reba's part about how her younger daughter Joanne was forever leaving her wallet around the house; once Reba had looked in it, did not see any money, then put it in Joanne's room. When Joanne came home, she "raised a fuss," and said her mother must have taken the money. She later found it tucked in a corner of the wallet. Reba was then reminded of an incident in which a wallet had been left in a bar where she and her friend were sitting; six people had looked in it and found nothing. Then Reba picked it up, took it into the ladies' room and found 40 dollars folded up in a corner of it. A windfall! They had a good time that night, and she had enough left over to buy her husband a pair of slippers.

They seemed to be involved in a kind of "shell game" with money; the drama and excitement that comes with losing, then gaining, something of value is the secret of gambling. In another social context, Reba might be describing a night at the gaming table. Having little excitement and less hope, the poor need to feel the freedom that comes with taking risks, just as the wealthy do. This explains the popularity of the "numbers game." Money symbolizes life chances; your attitude toward life is reflected in the way you handle money. What you do with it is your own business, as long as someone else has no real claim on it; and money that by chance comes one's way is readily appropriated without worry and guilt.

Learning Obedience and Responsibility: Harriet; Lucille   To steal outright is another matter. Harriet became incensed when Daniel took money out of her purse and Carla would not admit that he took it. She knew she had almost a dollar's change in her purse, but when she reached for carfare, she had only twenty cents. The downstairs neighbor told her that Daniel had almost a dollar in change. Harriet knew this had been going on for some time; sometimes Daniel did not bring back the change when she sent him for something. She was so angry she did not know what to do. Lucille told Harriet that she had the same trouble with Robert until he outgrew it.

Harriet relied a great deal on neighbors and friends in keeping up with her children's activities; she also depended on their squealing on each other. Usually they did; their failure to do so in this case was threatening to her system of child-rearing. Because they were so mutually dependent, their loyalty to each other was getting in the way of their responsibility to her. They were home alone all day during summer vacation while she was working. She made it a rule that they had to stay in until one o'clock; then they could go out and stay out until she got home. If she had not made that rule they would have gone out when they first got up and stayed out all day. She gave Daniel a key so he could let Carla in to go to the bathroom. He prepared sandwiches for their lunch. And they were not allowed to have any friends in the house when she was not home. As soon as she got home, their neighbor's children were at the door, asking for Daniel and Carla. Thus, she knew they must be obeying her, although she was aware that there was plenty of scope for secret disobedience. That was the root of her extreme anger when she discovered what she felt to be their treachery: she felt she was losing control, with dire consequences for herself and her children.

After Harriet moved to the high-rise apartments, she was especially strict about playing in the hallways and elevators. She also made sure that she knew where Daniel and Carla were and that the mothers of the children they played with knew where their children were. She did not want any trouble so that she might be asked to leave the building.

When Harriet took her children to visit Lucille, the two exchanged notes on bringing up their children. Harriet was scolding Daniel and Carla about their table manners and Lucille asked her, "Do you yell?" Harriet answered, "Yes, all day long." Lucille admitted, "I do, too. Sometimes I think it's not doing any good, but someone said, 'Maybe when they're thirty years old they'll remember.'" Being in rather unusual circumstances, because she and Harriet had never before visited with their children, Lucille was in an objective mood. After all, perhaps it was not so much what one said, but that one had something to say to one's children that counted. Lucille was amused when Harriet offered a prize to the child who ate in the best manner. She reported, "I guess she gave the prize to Arnold, although I don't know why: they were all doing the same."

Actually, Harriet gave them all money; when Arnold asked Lucille for permission to go to the store, she said, "No, you don't need to eat any junk." But Harriet said Daniel could go, and Arnold informed Lucille he was going along with Daniel and Carla. Lucille let it pass, to be polite in company, but she told him not to buy anything. After he left she said, "I know he'll spend some money."

Lucille complained that Arnold often only heard what he wanted to hear. I was taking him to the beach one day with some other children, and did not know that Lucille had given him strict orders on the phone to wait at home until she got back. When I arrived, he said nothing about waiting, so we drove on to the home of his friends; there we discovered that Lucille had already picked them up. When we returned, Lucille asked Arnold, "Did you hear Joyce on the phone when she said she'd take you swimming?" He nodded. "Did you hear what I told you on the phone, then?" He looked blank. "Oh, you can't talk now; you just pay attention to what you want to hear, what benefits you."

Lucille had not told Arnold why we should wait, but expected him to obey her implicitly. Obedience was important; he could figure out the reasons for himself.

Lucille complained that Arnold was getting more disobedient, but Robert's attitude was getting steadily worse. Arnold was her favorite; Robert was getting too big and acting too independent to be in her favor. When Robert, Arnold, Lucille, and I were dancing in her livingroom one time, "acting like fools," as she put it, Arnold remarked that Robert used to be ashamed, but now was not afraid to cut loose. Lucille said, "I don't like the way he dances: he moves around too much. Arnold is really the dancer." When Arnold came up to her and kissed her, she would say, "Arnie loves his mother." With Robert it was a love-hate relationship, with hate sometimes appearing to outweigh love.

Being Motivated   Harriet's children were still young and very dependent on her, but she gave them much responsibility at home. Both answered the phone and took messages in a polite, efficient manner. When Daniel did something for her, he usually handled it in a business-like way.

When Carla grew up, she could be a nurse; there was plenty of demand for nurses, Harriet thought. Of course, if she wanted to do something else, Harriet would not stop her. She did not know what she would like Daniel to be when he grew up, only that it should be something with a good salary. He could be a carpenter, since he liked to take things apart and put them back together. Or, she said jokingly, he could be a junk man, since he brings anything off the street. He was having trouble at school, especially with math. Harriet could not help him much,

because she did not understand the new math. He was not learning his multiplica-
tion tables like he should, either; she made him stay in to work on them, but she did
not believe he was really working.

When Daniel did pick up something quickly, such as when he began to draw
genealogical charts rapidly and accurately while his mother was being interviewed,
Harriet tended to disparage it. She remarked that he did not really understand
what he was doing; it was merely like drawing a picture. On another occasion, after
watching some bongo drummers at the beach, Daniel broke off two large sticks
and started hitting them together rhythmically. After a while, Harriet scolded him
and told him to stop. He also showed a great deal of independence on that day,
choosing his own routes along the shore and absenting himself from the rest of the
party for long periods of time. He was learning the "proper" male responses to
attempts by females to dominate him, developing an autonomous realm of his own
where they cannot follow, and which, complain as they may, they can do little to
change.

Daniel is said to be very slow in school, with the implication that he has a low
potential. On the other hand, Arnold is said to be underachieving. He is more
aggressive than Daniel and is not afraid to ask questions. Rather than copying the
genealogy, he asked me about the symbols. When I took him to the Museum of
Science and Industry, he asked me and the attendants many questions about the
displays. But Daniel has had much responsibility at an early age, and his impulses
have been checked in the interests of family integrity. Nevertheless, both Arnold
and Daniel have mastered their respective worlds and operate effectively within
them. While Harriet did not encourage Daniel to express himself, except in limited
ways, she was still teaching him skills and values that would be to his benefit later
on and was sending him to a school where he could become aware of opportunities
outside his world.

Getting into Trouble: Cluny James   Some mothers do not demand as much of
their children's time and attention as Lucille and Harriet do, nor can they give them
as much. Cluny James, the mother of twelve, worked hard to give her children what
they needed; when her youngest children were small, she managed to find a night
job so that she could take care of the little ones during the day. She did not want
to make the older children babysit with the young ones, so that they would say
when they grew up: "If it wasn't for Mother, I could have done so and so . . ." Then,
when they were all older, she worked in a restaurant owned by a friend who was
sympathetic. If she called home and one of the girls reported that the children were
doing something they should not be doing, her boss, a woman, took her home and
Cluny spanked all of them: she would not slight any of them when it came to
punishment.

Cluny James never had any trouble with any of her children until they moved
to Chicago. They had lived in a small town in Southern Illinois, and her husband
had provided well for them until he got "woman crazy" and left. They had a small
trucking business, transporting produce; she always had a big garden, so they had
plenty to eat. After her husband left, the older children wanted to move to Chicago;
she did not want to move, but finally consented. Life in the city was a struggle, and
some of the younger children began to get into trouble. She questioned her

decision to move and thought longingly about her garden and the peace of a small town.

The first time Cluny's children got into trouble, four of the boys came running home, very excited, and told her not to go outside. But she did go out and found a large group of people, mostly adults, with weapons of various kinds: one even brandished a rifle. She pushed it away from her and demanded to know what had happened; she was finally told that the children had had some kind of trouble in the "Y" and that it was her boys' fault. She said, "For heavens' sake, call the police; we can't handle it this way." She could not understand grown people "getting all worked up over children's doings."

Cluny told her neighbors to hit her children if they ever saw them doing anything wrong, like going out into the street. She could not be with them all the time, and the neighbors would not really harm them by hitting them, but the cars might. She never worried about anyone harming her children; she trusted her neighbors, just as she had at home. But in the city some people did not understand or believe in trust: it was one family against another.

Kenneth, her fourth youngest child, was taken to the police station for stealing when he was in high school. The police called and told her that they were holding her son, Kenneth, at the station. She replied, "Oh, no you aren't. My son is in school." But they had him; he had been arrested by the officer on guard at school for picking up a knife and a wallet that fell out of a boy's pocket in gym class. He shouted, "Here's a knife," holding it up. The boy denied ownership of the knife and accused Kenneth of taking his wallet. The officer spotted Kenneth as a potential troublemaker and arrested him; they booked him for stealing. Cluny scolded her son for being so naive and for not minding his own business. In effect, she told him to "see no evil, hear no evil, and speak no evil."

Kenneth learned that lesson, but he kept getting into trouble anyway. With police stationed in the schools, anything that happened between the youngsters threatened to become a criminal case. So, to his mother's dismay, Kenneth was on the way to having a police record. However, she could take solace in the fact that her oldest sons seemed to have settled down and her younger two had escaped most of the trouble that seemed to follow Kenneth. Only Kenneth and two of the others were causing her anguish. Louis, the second youngest, was doing very well in school; he was planning to go on to college and perhaps to become a priest. Street life did not appeal to him, and he left it alone.

When Kenneth was older, after benefit of psychologists, counselors, and priest, he got a job at a Neighborhood Youth Center—one among the many scattered throughout the city's poorer neighborhoods—on the South Side. There, children competed in various sports and games and learned the rules of group behavior from their peers and from the adults who were in charge. Their activities were supervised, but not as restricted as those of Daniel, Carla, and Arnold. They learned to fight and jostle each other in the group to which they all belonged.

Kenneth enjoyed his work at the Center; but at times he wondered if there would be a place for these children as they grew up, or even for himself when he outgrew this job. Certainly, the children did not know, although they spent their young lives trying to find their place.

REFLECTIONS ON "SAVE THE CHILDREN"

In order to be effective in achieving advantageous social arrangements, Black youth learn early to exercise their intelligence and will in a social context and to cooperate without being easily controlled or intimidated. Compromises must be made, but capitulation is disapproved; therefore, a child should be firmly disciplined but not suppressed. The apparent arbitrary character of parental discipline reflects the attitude that imparting awareness of and respect for social rules rather than the rationale behind such rules is the crucial factor in bringing up children. Reasons come through experience and maturation; and Blacks are painfully aware of the essentially arbitrary nature of much social rationalization.

In extended families there are adults—grandparents, aunts and uncles, step-father, or one or the other parent—who are in a relatively permissive relationship with children, which compensates for the usual rigorous discipline of the parental role. Further, an effective disciplinarian, such as Adrienne's mother, knows that treating a child as an equal on occasion will increase confidence and acceptance of authority. Through a judicious application of these techniques and through a close relationship with benevolent adults, a child comes to accept an authority whose effectiveness he can perceive.

The practice of "telling on each other" among siblings is encouraged by parents who must work; this tends to lessen solidarity among siblings and may add to sibling rivalry. However, it is an effective device in keeping children from con-spiring against absent adults and in controlling their behavior. It also serves as a means of social control in adult life (See Chapter 2, "Men and Women"), as does gossip in any community, and given the limited space in households, it may account for the stress on privacy with regard to one's personal business, as a self-defense.

In those families in which grandparents take responsibility for grandchildren, there is a tendency toward merging adjacent (grandparent-parent-child) genera-tions; this trend is in structural opposition toward merging alternate generations, which is more commonly found in kinship systems. Here the two opposing tend-encies result in a complex of role relationships depending, in each instance, upon which predominates. In Chapters 2 and 4 we see parents temporarily playing a "sibling" role in relation to one or more of their children (Adrienne and her hus-band; Eloise), while at a later time or with other children they assume a parental role. Alternatively, mothers and daughters may relate like siblings (Rachel and her mother; Diana and her child's paternal grandmother), both assuming a parental role toward their respective children and grandchildren; at other times daughters identify with their children vis-à-vis their own mothers.[2] These relationships are reflected in kinship terminological usage (See Chapter 3, "A Welcome Addition").

In the Black families described here, the social roles of breadwinner, discipli-narian, mentor, cook, and housekeeper may be assumed by people in a number of kinship statuses. These circumstances, together with the variations in adult-child

---

[2] Rainwater (1965) describes similar patterns among mothers and daughters in St. Louis, but regards them as indicative of family disorganization and lack of parental control, an assumption that is not made here.

roles, encourage a grasp of complexities in role relationships, division of labor, and of social process generally among Black children which stands them in good stead later on in relating to their contemporaries.

A problem faced by Black youth is their exposure to several sets of rules often conflicting. Each code carries its own definition of "responsibility." In the family, it comprises obedience, sharing, respect; among peers it entails generosity, daring, competition; and in the larger society—as interpreted by many Black parents—it means respectability, self-reliance, and thrift. Some mothers, like Lucille and Harriet, try to minimize conflicts by limiting their children's contacts with peers and by attempting to socialize them through precept and discipline to the values they feel they will need in later life. But since boys and girls must become men and women through testing and finding themselves among their peers, this strategy may result in rebellion and confusion. Encountering rejection from the larger society, young people may reject, in turn, the values learned at home and become alienated from their own communities. In an attempt to span the gap between an identity learned in family and community and an often frustrating and bewildering world, Black youth identify with culture heroes and heroines such as Jesse Jackson, Fred Hampton, and Angela Davis, asserting, "I am Somebody!" and then hope that someone is listening.

5 / Young, gifted, and black

INTRODUCTION

I play it cool
and dig all jive.
That's the reason
I stay alive.
My motto,
As I live and learn,
          is:
"Dig and Be Dug
In Return."

"Motto"
Langston Hughes

Your door is shut against my tightened face,
And I am sharp as steel with discontent;
But I possess the courage and the grace
To bear my anger proudly and unbent.
The pavement slabs burn loose beneath my feet,
A chafing savage, down the decent street;
And passion rends my vitals as I pass,
Where boldly shines your shuttered door of glass.
Oh, I must search for wisdom every hour
Deep in my wrathful bosom sore and raw,
And find in it the superhuman power
To hold me to the letter of your law!
Oh, I must keep my heart inviolate
Against the potent poison of your hate.

"The White House"
Claude McKay

MEMPHIS BLUES

The Urge To Create: Charles Raymond Chicago is a city of hustlers; from top
to bottom, from mayor to janitor, whether the hustle is running the show, running
as courier, holding down two jobs, having a man on the side, or cornering the

Reprinted from *Soulscript, Afro-American Poetry*, ed. June Jordan. New York: Doubleday, 1970.

Now, where?

market in some area of academia, Chicagoans keep up a fast pace in order to maintain a niche in their swiftly moving, intensely human city.

Charles Raymond moved to Chicago from Memphis with his parents when he was nine. They did not like Chicago and moved back to Memphis; about ten years later his brother returned to Chicago, and Charles visited him over vacation. His brother stayed only about two months and moved back home, but Charles looked up at the buildings and around at the city and decided he just had to stay. He was "scuffling," a less aggressive, Southern variant of "hustling," and the city seemed to challenge him with its aura of wealth and success.

Charles walked and walked all over the city, looking for a job; he finally found one with Western Electric. He married and had two children; but he felt a striving for recognition and success that pulled him away from his family into a private world of dreams and self-communion. He separated from his wife and started to attend college, majoring in music; he quickly learned to read and write music and to play several musical instruments. He wanted to write everything: all kinds of music, songs, short plays. He described a book he was writing:

It's about two young men—no, really one—who won the Heisman trophy in football. He was an artist, but always wanted to play football. He was too small— my build. A close friend of his—they grew up together—played football. They both won a scholarship to college and were roommates. The coach invented a system that was supposed to win all the games; the friend had to do extra practice, and used to work out with his roommate. They practiced together, and his friend learned all the plays. In one game, the friend was killed while making one of the plays; the coach came to his roommate to talk about how sad it was and he discovered that he knew all the plays. So he took his friend's place and executed all the plays well, so that he became a great player. I dreamed the whole thing.

Charles felt that the best time to create was when you were asleep; only then did you have complete solitude. He claimed to have dreamed all his songs completely, then he got up and wrote them down. He also painted, although he only did this when he was in the mood, so it took a long time to finish a picture. He painted one on a sheet and someone offered him 50 dollars for it, but he would not sell it. Then someone stole it.

A Family Heritage   Charles' greatest aptitude was for music. He came from a long line of musicians and felt confident that a great place was assured him in this field. His mother was a Dandridge, distantly related to Dorothy Dandridge, and her father had been "Buck" of the "Buck 'n' Bubbles" team; he played the piano and sang while his partner tap danced. Charles had seen them in an old Shirley Temple show, and recently, Bubbles had appeared on the Steve Allen show. Allen had played the part of Buck, who was dead; he had played the piano in the old style and reminisced. Charles' mother's brother and her sister's husband were also musicians and played with W. C. Handy, "Creator of the blues"; they had both played several instruments. It was a distinctive record of achievement, and it was little wonder that Charles, too, was highly motivated.

The musical association was still very strong among other family members as well. Charles' brother and sister and his mother's younger brother used to sing on the radio every Sunday, until his sister became pregnant. Charles sang in the church choir every Sunday, and his brother sang with a spiritual group, which later turned to rock 'n' roll. His brother wrote songs for the group. Charles traveled with the group in his brother's place once for two weeks. They went to New York and Washington, and he made 400 dollars a week. When he returned to Chicago, he joined a similar group and began to write music for them.

Charles' music was very original; he could not copy someone else if he tried. He was offered a contract for 30 percent of everything he wrote in the next seven years, but he refused, saying that he needed to be in a better bargaining position. He was sure to make a million!

He could hear every part of the music, every instrument, but he could not write it all down. He attended the Music Institute, and concentrated on music theory. He left the room he had rented in Hyde Park, where he was interrupted at all hours by friends stopping by, and moved to the YMCA downtown. There no one disturbed him and he felt more in the heart of the city, near the music school, the symphony, and the opera. He was growing excited about classical music; he had always liked Pop music, although he had never particularly liked the Blues, for which Memphis was famous. His style was more reserved and cool. He thought perhaps it was because his mother was from Boston.

Sometimes, when he went home, Charles' mother got sentimental and talked about the time her parents were in show business. Her mother was a singer, a beautiful, light-skinned lady who could pass for White. At first she gave up show business to take care of her family; but later, when Charles' mother was in her teens, she went on the road with her husband. Charles' mother and her brother lived with an older married sister. She met and married Charles' father when she was sixteen and he was eighteen, although her older sister objected. When Charles' grandmother returned, her daughter was married and about to have a baby.

Charles' parents had stayed together thirty years and had ten children. His mother's family had moved to California while Charles was quite young, leaving his mother, a younger brother, and a married sister in Memphis. The two sisters, Charles' mother and aunt, were very close, and the California relatives wrote often and occasionally came for a visit. Charles' mother adopted her husband's family as her own; they all lived nearby—his "Grandaddy" and grandmother lived right around the corner. Everyone called Charles' grandmother "Miss Daily"; she still called her husband "Mr. Raymond," because they had courted for such a long time.

The Demands of Manhood   Charles' father often reflected about how different things were when he was a child. They were very poor; he had to quit school in the sixth grade to take a job delivering groceries. He talked about how he got holes in his shoes from walking. He used to pray that things would be better for his children.

Charles was proud of his father: he was a real man. He was not working now, because he had diabetes. Charles, however, did not really believe that this was the reason, he thought he just did not want to work. He had worked hard all his life, even though he did not like working. Charles was very much like his father in this respect; he did not enjoy work, either, although he had held a job since his senior year. At present, he was drawing unemployment compensation while working as a waiter.

He was very much like his father in other ways, too. He liked to socialize, to listen to ball games and the news, and to read the papers every day. But he was not mean, as his father was sometimes; his sisters had acquired that mean streak. He also had some of his mother's traits, such as a love of cleanliness and neatness. He still kept his room extremely neat, although sometimes it was difficult; at home his sisters always cleaned everything up; they all just left the dishes where they were and the girls took care of them.

Charles felt that children were influenced by both parents, although the time of the year, the way the stars were, and when one was born were all important factors. Charles was convinced of the importance of the influence of the stars beyond a shadow of a doubt. One of his brothers was a Taurus and he was very stubborn; the other was a Pisces and he had a good memory. Neither of them knew anything about astrology. He read about his sign, Aquarius, and it was real, it was him. This was the Age of Aquarius, and he was sure that his dreams were destined to be fulfilled.

When Charles was growing up, Memphis was like a small town. It was much closer to nature: they lived adjacent to the river and there were trees and children could have dogs for pets. His paternal grandparents lived nearby, and whenever he visited them, his grandmother always insisted that he stay for dinner. His parents spent a lot of time with them, too. One of Charles' father's brothers was about his own age, and he and Charles socialized together frequently.

Charles was closest to his older brother, who was three years older than he. It was his brother who got him interested in music, and started him on his "career" of fatherhood. Charles had fathered in all five children by three mothers; he married the mother of the youngest two, but he did not get along with her at all. He had almost married the other girls, too; when he finally did marry, he found it was a mistake. Some people seemed to think he was terrible: "All those beautiful children. . ." and he used to feel bad, but now he did not feel anything. He had to live his own life.

The mother of his oldest children later married and had other children. His son and daughter wrote to him still, although he had not seen them for six years. His oldest daughter is about the age of his youngest brother. He recalled how his parents had found out about his escapade:

> It was so funny when Lottie's sister came over and told my parents, "So and so got my sister pregnant," and my father said, "He did wha-a-a-t?" I was in the bathroom; I cut out the window and left. I remember my mother said, "He'll take care of it, don't worry . . ." My mother was pregnant with (my youngest brother) when Lottie's sister came over to tell them. It was so damn funny, there my mother was poking out with my brother when she comes to tell her what her son had done.

After Lottie became pregnant, the two broke up; later they went back together again and she became pregnant a second time; Charles' oldest children, a boy and a girl, are two years apart. Then, a year after the second child was born, Charles had a son by another girl, who has also married since and had other children. A year later he impregnated his present wife, from whom he was now seeking a divorce. His second child by her was born two years after the first. Charles' mission, he said, was "to spread cheer," and he felt it was accomplished. Recently he had been seeing a young girl whose mother did not allow her to stay out late, so he decided he had enough of young girls.

Charles tried to be a father to his youngest children. He visited them once a week, although he felt that was not enough. He took them to the movies or shopping:

> They are really something: especially my little girl. She wanted everything in the store. I said, "You can't have everything; besides, what would you do with a baseball bat?" She got so mad at me: she wouldn't speak to me for two hours. I'll be glad when they get older so they can understand what I tell them. I really try to handle them.

Charles managed to return home once or twice a year to see his own parents, whenever he had the money. Three of his aunts (his father's sisters), live in Chicago; he had stayed with one of them for awhile when he first arrived, and she worried about him. She said she did not think he should be living alone. He tried to get over to see her occasionally, but he was always busy. He wanted to go back to Memphis eventually, but planned to travel first, especially to California and New York. He wanted to see his mother's family in California; he would like to be closer with them, but the physical distance keeps them apart. The last time Charles visited Memphis, his mother's oldest brother was arriving just as he was leaving. They talked to each other a long time on the phone and they cried from joy of speaking to each other.

Despite his "cool" demeanor, Charles could be very sentimental:

> The last time I was home, I saw my sister walking down the street, all dressed up for church, and I cried. She didn't see me . . . I remembered how when I was little she always went to church, every Sunday, and how I'd cut out the back way and wouldn't go. I didn't go for that, church and all. It's such a shame, our

family is so close and little things keep getting in the way and separating us . . .
someone marries and moves away . . .

Another Dream Deferred   Charles missed his family in Memphis, but his dreams
of glory and greatness were based in Chicago. While he was living in Hyde Park, I
was introduced to him by a friend of his who refused to be interviewed and who
thought that Charles might be more willing to pour out his feelings and ideas to a
sympathetic ear. A young girl once said to me, most young men "don't have the
time," but Charles needed someone to listen.

The last time I saw Charles, he was looking for one of his friends; he said he was
about to make his fortune and wanted to share it with him. He was going to
travel and wanted his friend to go along. Charles was high on drugs and dreams and
his head was in the stars that evening. Later, his friends reported that he had "gone
off the deep end," or "cracked up," using some such phrase, and I never heard
from him again.

A young man who was more secure than Charles reflected:

You should know my family: there are eighteen of us, all living—nine boys and
nine girls. And we're close as we can be—I can speak for all the rest of them,
too; maybe you think that's strange, but I can. My mother is forty-six and she
doesn't have to do a thing but live out her life to the fullest extent. We all
take care of her.

Charles had left the support and solace of his family to further his ambition; his
personal resources were insufficient, and he stumbled in the face of the constant
battles and reverses of the "high life."

A LIBERAL EDUCATION

The Classroom off the Street   On Wacker Street, across the Chicago River from
the Merchandise Mart, is a twelve-story edifice housing Central YMCA College. It
looks like any office building, but the business that is conducted within its walls is
quite different from that in other buildings around; it is higher education, plain,
unadulterated, and without benefit of arch and grassy mall. There, young men and
women from poor backgrounds come in to catch a glimpse of how the other side
lives and spends its time; and they are given a chance to enter the world of the
college-educated, if they are not discouraged or scared away.

Central offers a two-year Associate of Arts degree; its goal is to prepare its
students to enter a four-year college. Otherwise, they will fade back into the ranks
of labor or of the idle, with only a frustrating taste of liberation. Most of the
students work part time or full time, and most stay more than two years, unless
they drop out early. Many of them have trouble with their course work so that it
takes longer to get a degree; others have found a niche there and want to stay.
Carlos Williams, who was working as an advisor while taking advanced courses,
was one of the latter. He enjoyed his work and school, but he was wary of the
competition he would have to face in a four-year college. At Central he knew
everyone, he was doing fairly well, and he did not have to change his values
radically in order to achieve a measure of security.

The problem for Carlos was: Where could he go when Central no longer had a place for him? He was thirty-two, and his life style was fairly well set. He had grown up in the streets and had gotten into his share of trouble, having done a stretch in prison for killing a man. Three men had jumped him, but he had held a knife on them. He had paid dearly for his savage defense, but he was alive and whole. He still carried a knife and turned his back on no man. And he did not care to go into situations he knew nothing about.

The "Good Life": Carlos   Carlos yearned to live well; he enjoyed fine clothes, good food and drink, and pleasant surroundings. He had some hustles going for him, some involved women and others involved masculine activities such as gambling and occasional purveying of "hot" items. He shared his good fortune with his friends, and when hard times came, he could usually depend on them.

He had been married once, briefly, but did not get along at all with his wife. His last "woman," Sandra, was a pretty young girl, who could pass for White. They lived together for a time and she "turned tricks" for him now and then. She was a hard and angry young girl, but she loved Carlos. She became very dependent on him. He became angry because she refused to do anything for herself: She was a messy housekeeper, she would not go to school, and she wanted to "lay around and do nothing all day." Carlos tried to motivate her. He did not want her to just give up on life. During one of their quarrels she attacked him with a knife, and so he moved out.

Living alone, Carlos was able to keep his apartment as he wanted it; he was a good cook and liked to prepare "soul food," especially a good pot of "chitlin's." He was free to have as many women there as he wished; he had his share of them, but tried to keep from getting into another dependency relationship like the one he had with Sandra. He could be "slick" with women. Once he had three women in his apartment at the same time: they all knew each other and each thought that she was the only one with whom he had been intimate. He played the game well until the secret came out, and then he was in trouble. But he enjoyed the situation, particularly since one of his buddies had dropped by to see the show. They had all discussed the matter for awhile, attempting to be "cool" and "adult," then two of the girls left, in anger.

One of the three girls at the apartment that day was one of the teachers at Central, with whom Carlos had become friendly. She was a married woman, White, who was a graduate of a prominent Eastern Girls' college. He enjoyed her intellectual conversation and wit as well as her considerable physical endowments; also, she was trying to get him connections at another school. When she discovered that he was seeing several women, including one of her students, she reacted violently. She said that she was in love with him and he had led her to believe that he was in love with her, too. After that, she refused to speak to him, and she certainly did not try to help him. She had no intention of giving up her marriage for him, but it angered her that he was so free with his attentions. He rationalized his actions by saying that he had not been honest with her because she had not been honest with him.

The other two women were Black; they were also angry, but neither was particularly surprised. The one who had been a virgin when she first met Carlos claimed more contempt than she really felt, he thought. A few days later, she returned to his apartment where she watched television. Her legs were sprawled and he thought she was giving him the "come-on"; she denied this, and he asked her to leave. He was not going to play games with her; he liked to "rap" with women and was a master at "signifying,"[1] when the time was right, but when it came time to act, he did not fool around.

Carlos knew his world thoroughly and operated well in a rather free-swinging way, but he also had serious aspirations. He wrote poetry and had published a few poems in newspapers and periodicals. His father's uncle had been a famous poet. Also, Carlos had been a surgical technician during the Korean War and knew a great deal about human anatomy. He had thought about becoming a doctor, but realized that from a practical viewpoint it was impossible. It was hard for any Black man to enter the medical profession, but for Carlos to give up his nightlife and his freedom of thought and movement was unthinkable.

Carlos' mother and father were separated; he went to see his mother quite often and she called him nearly every day. He had never gotten along with his father. After he left Sandra, he had to raise a security deposit for a new apartment; he finally summoned enough courage to ask his father for it, as a last resort. He gave him the money. Carlos was trying to free himself from a woman, and his father helped as he would help a fellow sufferer rather than a son.

Carlos had been close to his grandfather—his mother's father; he called him "Daddy." When the old man died, Carlos and his mother and sister drove down to South Carolina to his funeral. But Carlos was angered and embarrassed by the behavior of his mother and sister. They seemed to be only concerned about what the old man had left and what they were getting from him. They did not seem to care at all about him as a person or mourn his death. Carlos told them what he thought about them; he decided to leave them there and fly back. He was able to obtain the money for his ticket from some of his relatives. He arrived home tired and depressed, only to find his apartment in disorder and Sandra ensconced on his sofa.

Sandra had been kicked out of her apartment and had nowhere to go. In a moment of weakness, Carlos had given her his key and told her to stay there and watch his things while he was gone. He had an expensive stereo and many books that he did not want to lose. But when he returned, he realized that it would not work: it just was not his place when Sandra was there. So he asked her to leave.

Sandra had been frantic when Carlos first left her. She begged him to come back: she would reform and would do anything for him. She came over to see him often and sometimes brought him money. She was still very much his woman, although he was dissatisfied with her and her way of life. Carlos was lonely; he felt he needed a "real" woman's love, not that of a child like Sandra. But all of the women he met were either after money or were too naive to relate to.

---

[1] I disagree with Kochman (see footnote 37, Chapter 7) that "to signify" always refers to an insult. Here, Carlos uses it to mean "engaging in making statements with double entendre, whose sexually suggestive, meaning is obvious to the person to whom one is speaking."

Carlos began to feel more and more depressed. At the same time, he was hard-pressed financially, because a loan he had applied for at school was delayed. He felt that it was deliberately kept from him by certain people at school; he knew them all well and was aware of much about their personal lives. He thought about his loneliness, his uncertain future, and about Sandra; his face began to swell up and he became alarmed. It had happened before, and the doctors had never been able to find any allergy. They put him in the hospital, and the doctors told him it was psychological.

After he got out, Carlos continued to be depressed. He thought about suicide; when he felt that way, he called someone to talk about it, even if it was the middle of the night.

Things got worse, and finally Carlos lost his apartment. He was not as free and independent as he would have liked to be; he and Sandra got back together. He was as dependent on her, it seemed, as she was on him. He was still critical of her, but he was worried about himself and desperately needed someone who cared. And she certainly did seem to care. As the song goes, "I may not be the one you want, but I'm the one you need."

A Failure of Education: Kenneth James   Carlos and Charles were basically art-ists: their frustrations were intensified by extreme sensitivity and awareness of past greatness. Kenneth James, on the other hand, was a young man who merely wanted an education and a reasonable degree of success. Yet for a young Black man, even this goal can impose much suffering and involve nearly insurmountable obstacles. He had been expelled from high school because he got into a fight with a fellow student, and seriously injured him. He later attended night school and received his diploma; but he never felt quite the same as if he had graduated with his class. He talked his teachers into waiving a class that he needed to graduate, and thus he somehow felt as though he had "tricked" his way through school. Although he had read and studied a lot when he was younger, the immediate pressure of becoming a man had interfered with school and he had not done so well. But when he found himself in the city with nowhere to go but down, he began to think seriously about going on to college.

Kenneth had some friends who were going to Central YMCA College; they told him about the Work-Study program with the Neighborhood Youth Centers. He talked to an older woman who was working there, and she encouraged him to apply. She introduced him to the Director and to some of the other Youth workers. Things went well, and Kenneth found his place there.

He enjoyed working at the Youth Center; he was in charge of the Game Room and supervised children from six to sixteen years of age. Kenneth came from a large family; his father left his mother with twelve children. He never really had time to be a child because of the emotional and physical demands of a large and impoverished family. His mother did her best to give her children every opportu-nity; but there were constant family crises, and Kenneth and his brothers and sisters were always ready to come to the aid of their mother or others in the family. Many times in his life Kenneth himself had been the recipient of the family help and con-cern. Too early, he was on the streets, trying to prove himself a man. Having missed his own childhood, he loved the children he worked with at the Center; he gave unsparingly of himself and experienced the thrills of learning new skills and abilities along with them.

Kenneth felt that he did not get the kind of support from his supervisors and the other workers at the Center that he needed; they were too concerned about programs and budgets and their personal lives to care much about the children. The game room had inadequate equipment, much of it dilapidated, and Kenneth finally complained. He did not quite dare to present his complaint in the form of a demand; he put it in as a recommendation in his yearly report. But little heed was paid to his suggestions, and Kenneth's frustration increased.

Meanwhile, Kenneth was being introduced to Freshman English and the Humanities at Central. It was felt that these courses were most crucial for children of the ghetto, who had little that was liberating in their backgrounds. The teachers undertook their mission with zeal; Ken's English teacher was a strict grammarian and marked grammatical errors on Freshman themes with enthusiasm. It made no difference how original an idea, or how much visible effort a theme had involved. She aimed for the essentials: the wrong verb tense, the misspelled word. With the unerring instinct of the self-chosen elite, she managed to set back most of her students several quarters, if she did not drive them out of school entirely.

Kenneth's Humanities teacher was less aggressive, but also less involved. He assigned the classics—Homer, Tacitus, Plato—with a generous concern for his students' lack of background. However, he neglected to relate the very human episodes hidden in the stilted translations to the experiences of his students. Understandably, they continued to languish in the desert of "cultural deprivation."

Some of Ken's teachers at Central were more sensitive to their students' needs than others. But none of them really inspired him; he was convinced neither of the importance and value of the subjects nor of the genuineness of his teachers' concern to teach. It all seemed unreal and irrelevant when measured against his family's crises and needs, the problems at the Center, and life on the streets. Ken was not acquitting himself well in school, and he was feeling more and more alienated from higher education. It appeared to be an extension of the frustration he had experienced in high school. If it were not for his attachment to the children at the Center, he probably would have dropped out.

Some of the Black students at Central, the more militant ones, formed a group that attempted to monitor the morals and activities of the others in order to maintain Black unity. They criticized Black students for spending too much time in the lounge, "BS-ing" and playing cards; they came out strongly against fraternization of Black and White students and stressed the seriousness of the vocation of the Black student. Some of the students were strengthened and motivated by this pressure; others, like Kenneth, were even further alienated. His deepest loyalties were to his family and boyhood friends; he could not identify with all Black people, in opposition to White. Many of the Black people he knew were much better off than he and his family; they seemed to be the ones who were making the most demands. They were not, he felt, his leaders. They were doing many of the things for which they criticized others and were benefitting from them. Kenneth distrusted anyone who tried to tell him what he should do; his commitment was to family and close friends.

None of Kenneth's older brothers or close friends was attending college; he had no one with whom he could talk about school, or to whom he could relate on a deep level in his daily activities at Central. This kind of identification was extremely important to Kenneth; he could not function effectively without it. The social climate at Central inhibited open relationships, and Kenneth was painfully sensitive to the hostilities that develop when people from widely differing backgrounds are thrown together and expected to produce a new and liberating experience with little leadership. He found real comradeship and liberal education on the streets, and this is where he fled when pressures began to converge on him.

"THE HOLE"

Home Away from Home   When Kenneth was fourteen, he went to live with his aunt, his father's sister, because he was constantly getting into trouble, and his mother had several small children to look after. His aunt was strict; she was extremely religious and would not allow smoking or drinking in her house. She was kind to Kenneth and in her way tried to help him, but he felt that there was really no place for him in her household. He began to spend more and more time on the streets.

About this time, Kenneth began to frequent a place popularly referred to as "The Hole." It was not a fancy place—just a bar and two or three booths with unsteady tables and sprung seats. Perhaps because of its lack of pretensions, as well as its location, it had become a refuge for those who for some reason or another felt that the world had passed them by.

The mood of "The Hole" changed with the hour. In the daytime, the customers were people who worked in businesses in the area; as they left, their places were taken by night people—pimps, prostitutes, homosexuals, and others who felt an antipathy toward daylight. The bartenders were all middle-aged, respectable men who maintained an atmosphere of decorum amid the occasional threat of anarchy that pervaded the bar.

Among the regular customers at "The Hole" was Jeanine Smith's brother, who was a Vietnam war veteran. When Jeanine was living at home, her brother had been a quiet youth. But since he came back from the war, he was hostile and argumentative. He still lived with his mother and stepfather in Mother Cabrini Greens, which was only a few blocks away. He could be seen in the bar frequently, arguing and threatening a fight.

Ernie Baker, another regular customer, was the jester of "The Hole." With a twist of his flexible physique and a turn of his quick tongue, he could turn impending ugliness into a joking exchange. Ernie had been a professional boxer until he had been injured in the ring and was forced to retire. Because of his background, he commanded a great deal of respect, despite his rather small size. While he did not actually brag about his record, he let it be known. People laughed at his antics, but were careful not to cross the fine line between humor and ridicule.

Kenneth saw Ernie occasionally in "The Hole," but when he first started going there he did not get too involved with the other customers. He merely sat and listened to the juke box and to the general conversation; he was lonely and lost. Then, at age eighteen, he met Florence, a woman in her late thirties who came into the bar after work in the evening. Florence was lonely, too; Kenneth, who sported a moustache, looked much older than his eighteen years. By the time Florence found out his real age, she and Kenneth were involved in an intense relationship.

An Older Woman   Kenneth spent weekends at Florence's home. She never went out on Saturday or Sunday except to buy the Sunday paper, to pick up a few groceries, or to replenish her stock of bourbon. Florence drank considerably, although it never interfered with her job or prevented her from functioning in any way. She kept a neat apartment and brought up her son, Toby, with care. Kenneth thought a great deal of little Toby, and loved him almost as if he were his own. In front of Toby, Florence referred to Kenneth as "Mr. James." She did not want him to know about their relationship. But Kenneth was sure that Toby knew.

Kenneth had worked at various jobs in his young life; when he was twelve or thirteen he delivered papers to the wealthy residents of the Gold Coast. His customers were housewives who were bored and frustrated. One day, he was seduced by one of them; after that experience, he was not backward about approaching an older woman when she looked at him in a certain way, regardless of her station. After he stopped working as a newsboy, Kenneth had several jobs: bus boy in a fancy restaurant; attendant at Marina City—the posh river resort in downtown Chicago; and other less glamorous jobs. He became a courier for the syndicate, delivering various "packages" for them; he lived in fine hotels and sported an expensive wardrobe. But he grew too old for the syndicate and too susceptible to arrest, so they dropped him. At eighteen, Kenneth lacked any real vocation, as well as a home.

His relationship with Florence gave Kenneth a measure of stability, although publicly they had little to do with one another. Florence held a rather responsible position and did not want it to be known that she was having an affair with a man so much younger than herself. But people in "The Hole" knew that they were together. Ernie Baker was attracted to Florence; he and Kenneth became acquainted when he sat down to have a friendly conversation with the two of them over coffee one night. Ken was surly because he felt that Ernie was trying to "get next to" Florence; Ernie was closer to Flo's age, and Kenneth felt insecure. But Ernie was friendly, and the two of them grew to be close; they really got into each other's "bag." Although he still liked Florence, Ernie never approached her, not even after Ken and Florence broke up.

Male Bonding   Ernie and Ken used to come into "The Hole" at all hours of the day and got to know a wide range of the clientele. Ernie had gone to Purdue for two years; he could communicate with all kinds of people—criminals, businessmen, wineheads, and intellectuals—with equal aplomb. He himself had known the academic life, a life of relative affluence, and the press of poverty. At the time he was working as a waiter; but his wife left him and he grew depressed, so he stopped working and began drinking excessively. He took up with a woman who seemed to satisfy his needs for awhile, but it did not work out, and he went on from one woman to another. Then he began to be seen frequently with whores and women of the moment. He talked more and got into some fights while he was drunk. People began to lose respect for him especially when he began to "leech off" them for his drinks.

Larry was another partner of Kenneth's, who took to drinking wine when his girlfriend left him. When Ken first knew him he was working as a waiter and was always dressed in a tuxedo; he carried a large bank roll at all times and demanded the finest of everything. But he fell in love with a White woman who would not marry him. After that Larry began to go down hill. He neglected his appearance—he did not bathe or care how he dressed.

Larry's only relatives in the city were a sister, who was always lecturing him, and an uncle, whom he seldom saw. Larry was not even informed about it when his uncle was in the hospital. He went to the hospital to see Ken's brother, who had pneumonia. When he walked into the semiprivate room, he saw his uncle in the next bed. The old man said, "Oh, you've come to see me?" and Larry looked foolish, saying that he was glad to see him but did not even know he was sick. He told his sister about it later, and laughed until it seemed that he was crying. He fell apart right there in front of his sister. She looked at him in a matter-of-fact way and invited him and friends to her birthday party in a few weeks. It was a real party, he told Ken later. His sister always had lively parties with plenty of booze and which lasted all night.

Ken felt sorry for his buddies: Ernie and Larry were rapidly deteriorating in front of him. Several times Larry said that if he could get his woman problems straightened out he would be all right. Ernie was a little older than Larry. Also, he had been married and had known relative success. Although he was going down hill, Ken felt he had the potential to pull himself out.

When Ken and Florence broke up, he was also in a deep state of depression for several months. He had been too insecure, too possessive, and as a result, he had lost her. She tired of his jealous scenes and violence and told him never to come around again. She had friends who would enforce her request with a gun, if need be. Ken reacted in a different way than did his partners, however; he took the job at the Center and went on to school. Sometimes he stayed in his room for days, reading, listening to music, and dreaming. He was crushed, and felt that he would never love again. But the optimism and strength of a young physique asserted itself and he began to see another woman, also older, with whom he was not in love. And so life continued for him.

Ken and Ernie began to drift apart; Ken remained loyal to Ernie, however, despite what people said. He also did what he could for Larry, although his own resources were limited. It was sobering to see what life had done to these men who were older than he. For the most part, his own older brothers were settled and had families, except for one who had run away from the city entirely. Ken was trying to reconcile the authority and sobriety of his older brothers with the freedom and sophistication he found in people in the street. Somehow, he did not feel that the latter should lose out without a struggle.

Kenneth was happy when he met Ernie one night and was informed that his wife had come back to him and that Ernie was going back to Purdue. He felt confident that Ernie would be successful; there was room for people like Ernie and himself, who did not quite fit into the mold, but were able to come back up from the bottom and "keep on keeping on."

REFLECTIONS ON "YOUNG, GIFTED, AND BLACK"

In Frederick Douglass' autobiography the intensive socialization and mutual support among Black men, which led to the emergence of leaders such as Douglass and other historical figures, is clearly evident as it is in the foregoing pages. Because they are Black, however, these young men deal with the severe handicaps of their environment without benefit of an *institutionalized* myth of male superiority, although they are sustained by bonds of friendship and kinship. If a Black man is able to survive and to overcome his problems, he is truly, in the idiom, "Together!"

6 / Reunion

INTRODUCTION

Observers of Black family life who characterize it as "adaptive" have not given sufficient weight to the time, expense, and energy invested in ritual activities such as reunions, funerals, and other celebrations. While these festivals indeed strengthen the system of economic reciprocity that prevails in Black communities, to label them as "adaptive" is surely to put undue emphasis on their narrowly instrumental aspects. They are, rather, a supreme expression of that system of exchange which, while reinforcing mutual aid among members, also signifies a social identification with a powerful group whose orientation is not merely one of survival, but of advancement through unity and mutual social support. Further, the ceremonies of the extended family are an embodiment of the drama, excitement, sociability, and display that are essential to the human spirit.

GETTING IT TOGETHER

The Social Life of Taverns   I met Ernestine at an affair sponsored by the West Side Women's Club, a crowded, lively party held in a large ballroom. A considerable amount of talent was displayed that night, both professional and amateur. The mistress of ceremonies was an announcer at a local Black station, and the entertainment ranged from singing, dancing, and comedy skits to an amateur-style show, where the audience judged the talent. This was an appropriate setting for my meeting with Ernestine; I later discovered, as I became involved in the planning and execution of the largest and most elaborate family reunion I have experienced, that when Ernestine and her family entertain themselves and others they spare neither energy nor talent. From the oldest grandmother to the smallest toddler, they all have an eye and a taste for the dramatic.

About a week after the Women's Club affair, Ernestine called and asked me to attend a birthday party given for a friend at a South Side tavern. I arrived at 11 P.M. and Ernestine was sitting at the bar, talking to her cousin, Arlen Collins. She was dressed in a pants suit with a large fur stole. She is a handsome woman and likes fine clothes, which she designs and makes herself. She showed me some pictures of herself in some of her outfits, taken by photographers in various night

Sophisticated lady

spots. She also had some pictures taken that night, standing tall and imposing, like a singer or other celebrity. Her sister, Margaret, remarked to me later, "Ernestine should have been a model."

The girl being feted that night arrived soon after I did; Ernestine had to leave about midnight to go to work and barely had time to wish her "Happy birthday." People were coming and going all evening, according to their work schedules, but in the informal atmosphere of the tavern, arrivals and departures were casual and unobtrusive.

Taverns play an important part in the social life of South Side, Chicago; birthday celebrations, reunions, even funerals are occasions upon which family and friends congregate in favorite places, to deal with life crises in a congenial atmosphere. They do not merely provide an escape from problems at home and at work, but are an important extension of social life as well. In taverns you meet people with a wide variety of experiences and greet old friends in pleasant surroundings. The bartenders, male and female, play an important role in a complex relationship among the regular customers, with others joining in to contribute to the evening's entertainment. The exchanges are usually humorous, sometimes pathetic, occasionally angry, but always very human. For example:

Old man (to bartendress): Dorothy, where's those pants you wore yesterday?
Bartendress: I like to wear a skirt sometimes; after all, I am a woman.

Old man: I'm glad you said that; I'm glad you're a woman and I'm a man.
(Laughter from others at bar)
Younger man: Yeah, a woman is a good thing; a little lovin' is a good thing.
Old man: I like a little lovin'; I can't take too much lovin', just a little lovin'.

In Elm Park, the suburb South of Chicago where Ernestine was brought up, the churches are strong and have managed to keep most taverns out. There are only two good taverns there. After Ernestine's Cousin Howard's wake, his relatives met in one of them to socialize and "let off steam" after the stuffy atmosphere of the funeral parlor. Ernestine met someone there whom she had known all her life, but whom she had not known was her cousin. He was also related to her sister Sally by marriage; Sally knew of the relationships, but Ernestine first learned of them that night in the local tavern, not an unlikely place to create a social bond where there was previously only a potential one. She had always liked Saul Robbins; now he was part of her family.

Long after Ernestine had lost touch with other cousins on her father's side, she used to see Cousin Irene and her husband, who own a restaurant and tavern. She used to stop by on her way to work for a cocktail with Cousin Irene. When she changed jobs, it was too far out of the way, so she stopped going. But she still feels closer to that cousin than to others on that side.

Introduction to the Reese Family On the evening of the birthday party, Ernestine's cousin, Arlen Collins, invited me to the Reese family reunion, which was to be held later in the summer. It was the fifth annual reunion of the descendants of Grandma and Grandpa Reese, and they were planning an "anniversary," a special celebration, for that year. Ernestine and Arlen, her mother's sister's son, were making most of the arrangements. At the time, Ernestine was working at two jobs and had two small children to take care of, but she still found time to plan and work on the reunion. It was important to Ernestine that the reunion be a success. It was a family affair, and what is more important than family? She told me that she felt sorry for people who did not have big families: how could they have any joy in life?

As the weeks passed, I learned about the history of the reunion. It was originally Cousin Ruby's idea. (Ruby is Arlen's sister and the oldest of the Collins branch of the Reese family.) Whenever there was a death in the family, there was a large gathering, and everyone was so happy to see everyone else; she thought it was a better idea to have a reunion on a happy occasion instead of a sad one. She sent out the invitations, but she could not do too much about organizing the affair because she had so many children and it was hard for her to get around. Therefore, her brother and oldest daughter have taken her place and they work with Ernestine in planning and organizing the event.

Ruby's mother, Oralee, died about 20 years ago; she had the most children of all the Reese brothers and sisters, leaving twelve children at her death. Oralee was the oldest surviving child; the second oldest, Ruth, had nine children. Oralee married a Collins; Ruth's married name was Davis. These two families, the Collins and Davis families, made up for all the others, who had few or no children. Two Reese children, a boy and a girl, died as babies; two girls died young without having

The old days

children and another died childless in later life. The two oldest living daughters, Rose and Nettie, have no children and one brother is childless. The remaining offspring of Grandma and Grandpa Reese, three sons and two daughters, have only two or three children apiece. Grandma Reese had fifteen children in all, and it was only among the Collins and Davis children and grandchildren that this tradition of a large family has been carried on. But these two branches, along with the normal addition of members through the generations, assure a heroic task for whoever attempts to get the Reeses together for a reunion.

As Ruth Davis' children grew up and married, they became active in the church and in other organizations. The Collins family was not as well known in the community; perhaps this is one reason why Ruby and Arlen, who are the most active of the Collins branch, started the reunions. At any rate, the impetus for an all-family affair came from the Collins side, while the Davises have often been instrumental in getting their cousins to attend social affairs in the community.

Ruth Davis' oldest daughter, Verona, is married to a bus driver for the Chicago Transit Authority. He is active in the CTA Club, which sponsors dances two or three times a year. He is quite a hustler and sells many tickets, some of which he sells to his wife's relatives. Verona and Roger are well liked by the young people, and members of the Davis and Collins families attend the dances. They come bringing food—potato salad, ham, and chicken—and a bottle of liquor, then order set-ups. There is plenty of entertainment and everyone has a good time. Before the reunions, that was the only time many of them saw each other during the year. But it got so crowded, they stopped attending as often; this was when Ruby thought about having an annual picnic for the family. They call it the Reese reunion, in honor of Grandma and Grandpa Reese, although there are Collins, Davis, Johnson, and many other family names represented there.

Ernestine does not remember much about her Grandfather Reese, but has seen pictures of him with a large, curving mustache, sitting in a high-backed chair: he looks just like a bishop. His relatives live in Cleveland, Ohio. There is a Reese reunion there, as well. This year Ernestine's mother, Sarah, three aunts, and some cousins from Chicago attended the Cleveland reunion and reported that they had a wonderful time. A Reese cousin on that side who was a social worker had planned the gathering. She decided to have one for the Western branch of the family, then another for the Eastern branch. The Chicago Reeses had stayed with some neighbors who lived in the same block as the Cleveland Reeses; they were treated as honored guests, and their cousins ordered a tray of hors d'oeuvres for their Sunday dinner. It must have cost at least $25.00!

The Reese family reunion in Chicago centers around the children of Grandma and Grandpa Reese and their families. Only one family, that of Cousin Joseph Collins, lives outside of Chicago and its environs; he lives in Detroit and gets to the family gathering only occasionally. Relatives by marriage may or may not come; they are not expected to come, but are welcome when they do. On the other hand, children, grandchildren, and great-grandchildren are expected to come, and they do, in large numbers. Ernestine and the others especially want to attract the young people to the reunion, since they ordinarily do not care for family affairs. Their presence and the desire to have them come greatly influences the planning of the program.

Ernestine's father does not come to the Reese reunions; neither do his sisters and brothers, although they grew up with the Reeses in Elm Park. Two cousins on that side are married to cousins on Ernestine's mother's side, so they are naturally invited.

The Johnsons   The cousins on Ernestine's father's side came to her sister, Susan's, wedding, but those on her mother's side did not. Susan had sent special invitations to each of her cousins on her father's side. On her mother's side, she sent only one invitation to all the aunts, and one invitation to all the children of each aunt; they were to notify each other. They felt that the invitation had been merely a formality and therefore did not come. Weddings are most important to the immediate family and are usually events at which the father's side is stressed, at least for the Reeses. Only a few of the older relatives represented the Reese side. It was not a large wedding, but Susan's mother baked a large cake and fixed a champagne fountain. Her in-laws think a lot of her and always like to come to any affair when she is responsible for the arrangements.

Sarah, Susan's and Ernestine's mother, is Ernest Johnson's second wife. He had three children by his first wife, two boys and a girl. The two boys were brought up by their mother's sister, and the girl stayed with her father, Ernest, and his second wife, Sarah. Ernestine is very close to her half-sister, Margaret, who was a little girl when her mother died. Margaret left home while Ernestine was still a child; she used to visit her in St. Louis and she would cry when it came time to go back home. She could talk to Margaret about things she could not tell her mother and felt closer to her than to her own younger sisters.

On Mother's Day every year Ernestine's immediate family has a gathering, and Margaret and her brothers all try to come. The oldest boy, Lawrence, works for the railroad; sometimes he can attend, depending on his schedule. Whenever he is in town, Ernestine's sisters go down to his hotel and take him out to Elm Park, or else he spends time with his mother's or his father's relatives. Last Mother's Day, the other brother, who does not see his family members often, could not get to the gathering, because he works in a tavern on the West Side and seldom gets holidays off. So his brothers and sisters went out to see him and they had a get-together at the tavern.

Margaret and her brothers usually do not come to the big Reese reunion. When Ruby sent out the invitations, she did not send them one because they are not Reeses. When Ernestine took over the invitations, she invited Margaret to the "anniversary" reunion, and Margaret came in from St. Louis.

"Catching Up" on Family: The Collins', The Davises, and the Irrepressible Aunts. Ernestine took her task of planning the anniversary reunion seriously. She was on the phone constantly, talking to relatives. She does not have a car and so she does not get out to Elm Park often, not even on holidays, when she usually has to work. She keeps in contact by phone, mostly through Cousin Anne, one of the Davis girls. The two are about the same age and have maintained their childhood friendship. Anne lives in Elm Park and keeps up on all the news: who is married, who has had a baby. She is very active in the church, which is the best source of information on people in Elm Park.

Ernestine grew up with two of the younger Collins girls, as well, but they have left Elm Park and she has lost touch with them. Since she became involved in the reunion she has had a lot of contact with Ruby and with Arlen Collins, although she had not been close with them while growing up. Ruby was older than she, and Arlen, of course, was a boy. They, like most of the other cousins, have moved from Elm Park and seldom get back. Many of the cousins work at two jobs, like Ernestine, and have little time to visit. They talk on the phone to those relatives to whom they are closest. Ernestine usually talks to Anne about twice a week, to her mother once a week, and occasionally to Aunt Rose. But when she began to work on the reunion, her telephone calls increased considerably and she went out to Elm Park more frequently. She began to be more conscious of family and to think of the Reese family as a whole. Her basic objectivity, developed through years of experience and independence, asserted itself and was focused on her family. Gradually, Ernestine took hold.

I was working on Ernestine's genealogy at the time; she decided to make up programs for the reunion using the genealogical information. She had a page for each family, listing all the Reeses and their descendants. This entailed many telephone calls and two trips out to Elm Park as well as one to Ruby's house in order to get all the names right. We went out to the old Reese homestead, a lovely, roomy old house. The walls were lined with pictures and with memories, and there I met Aunt Rose, who was a magnetic woman of seventy years plus, and Aunt

Nettie, who was lively and deliberately droll. Uncle Alfred was fixing the chandelier for his sisters when we arrived; he lives in a basement apartment downstairs. He inquired about the genealogy, what good it was going to do for them, and I had to confess that I did not know.

We had picked Anne up at her house, which was on the way, and brought her with us. She contributed all the information for the Davises in her very efficient club-church-woman manner. She had done a lot of homework. Then Rose gave us information about the older generation, people whom Ernestine did not know or did not know were related. Nettie interrupted from time to time, confusing Rose and teasing her about her lack of knowledge about her own kin. But Rose did not seem to mind.

Rose had recently been forced to retire from her job as cook at the County Hospital due to a bad leg; still, she had just returned from an all-day shopping trip, on foot. She had been looking unsuccessfully for a pair of gold slippers to wear to Ernestine's parents' fiftieth anniversary celebration, at which she and Nettie were going to be attendants; she decided to wear the silver shoes she already had. She told us that last week she and Nettie, looking for something to wear to the golden wedding celebration, had gotten down a lot of old clothes from the attic, including costumes they used to wear as "The Reese sisters," a singing group. It was easy to picture Nettie clowning around in the costumes and fancy dresses they had brought down. Nettie had found a green dress she had worn on tour when she was a professional singer; she declared she was going to wear that, so the other attendants all had to buy or make green dresses for the celebration.

Rose and Nettie recalled their own parents' fiftieth anniversary celebration, which they described in glowing and extravagant terms. The house was overflowing with flowers and the important people of the community were all there, including the white people. They showed us a picture taken at that time: a dignified old couple, seated, with all their sons and daughters standing behind them. Ernestine and her sisters remember stopping in every day after school to help their grandmother get ready for the celebration. The two older women continued their reminiscences; I was attracted by their personalities and vivid recollections and felt reluctant to leave.

A week later, at Ruby's house, we sat around the big dining room table and caught up on the incredible Collins family. Five of Ruby's children were living at home, as well as four grandchildren. In addition, Ruby babysits for working mothers. I could fully understand why she had little time to work on the reunion.

Ruby could not remember some of the younger Collins members; her daughter, Sheila, helped out with these. Sheila and one of her sisters are married to brothers, but are living at their mother's house with their children. Ruby has had a playroom fixed up in the basement, but still the house seems crowded. It was incomprehensible to me, not belonging to a large family, that someone so constantly surrounded by family would initiate the idea of a family reunion. Ruby obviously needed to feel a part of a larger family group.

Divisive Tendencies: Sisters and Wives   The reunion was to be a picnic, held in a city park not far from Elm Park. They all had been dissatisfied with the arrangements for the last reunion, so one Sunday, Ernestine, Aunt Rose, and Aunt

Nettie, and Cousins Arlen, Ruby, and Anne went out to look at a new picnic site. There was considerable hilarity as they discussed Ruby's problem: she needed a U-Haul truck to get all her children there this year. Her husband never had a car and they could not manage to get rides with her brothers, so she had to rent a car.

On their way back they discussed the previous reunion, what they had not liked about it and who had not come. Several of the male cousins were not there. Howard Davis and his family had not been there; it was felt that his wife has kept him away from his brothers and sisters. He is a contractor and has done very well. His wife occasionally comes to family events just to make an appearance, but last year they did not come. Perhaps it was because Howard had been sickly.

In the case of Edward Davis, it was definitely his wife who kept him from coming. She is older than he, old-fashioned, and more like his mother than his wife. She does not trust his sisters. Perhaps she is afraid they will get him a date. One time when his oldest sister, Verona, went over to see him, his wife got angry and told her she did not want Edward's sisters in her house when she was not home. When Ernestine called Edward to come out to the reunion, he demurred, saying that his sisters did not like him; his wife was on the other phone and interrupted: "I want to know what's going on." When Ernestine explained, she said, "We won't be out there; Edward's sisters don't like *me*." Anne told Ernestine that Edward's wife says a lot of things she does not mean.

Another cousin, Arnold Collins, came but his wife did not. She is unfriendly to her in-laws and will not come to any family events. Arnold's brother, Raymond, is married to Vanessa, whose brother is also married to a Reese. Vanessa had some disagreement with Ruby and they did not come, either. Ruby insisted that Vanessa wanted to come, but that Raymond was just like his father, and hated reunions. Perhaps Vanessa did not feel she should come alone, since it was not her family, although her brother was there with his wife, a Collins.

There was a reluctance among closer relatives to admit these divisive elements among Reeses. They all agreed that it would be a more successful reunion if all the cousins were there and if those who came would cooperate more. They should all try to come at about the same time, Ernestine said, so they can have some group activities. Some come at noon, some do not come until four o'clock. By the time they eat and get to see everyone, it is time to go home.

This year they were going to introduce everyone so they would all know each other. They were going to have games and contests with prizes. Ruby's oldest daughter was going to get the prizes at the discount store where she works. She would also get pen and pencil sets for all the high school graduates. They would arrange for a disc jockey who would bring his own records and equipment. Since they had to pay him 40 dollars for the day, they were going to collect $2.00 from each family. Ernestine was to take charge of hiring the DJ; she would also buy decorations and help plan the program. She was so busy for a few days before the reunion that she did not go to work, forfeiting almost a week's salary.

About a month before the big day, Ernestine attended a Woman's Day service at the Baptist church in Elm Park. The guest speaker was the minister's wife. She spoke of cooperativeness and how women should work together in the church without jealousy. Often the minister praised some women who were quite active in the church and the others become envious. Anyway, Ernestine felt, it is the "silent worker," who does not talk about what she is doing but just does it quietly who accomplishes the most. Ernestine took the sermon seriously and renewed her resolution to stay above the conflicts and jealousies that inevitably result when a family comes together. In the remaining weeks, she dedicated herself to organizing a successful reunion.

THE REESE SISTERS

A Past To Be Proud Of Grandma and Grandpa Reese were among the pioneers in Elm Park. Ernestine remembers Grandpa Reese as a dignified, pleasant old man and Grandma Reese as quiet but likeable. She and her sisters enjoyed visiting their grandparents; they went there every Sunday after church. Grandma Reese went to church every Sunday until she could no longer get around; even after that, Ernestine recalls, she did all the cooking.

Grandma Reese's mother—Grandma Jones—lived to be 103. She outlived Grandpa Reese and stayed on with her daughter until her own death. Grandma Jones had lived during the days of slavery and once had told her grandchildren about how she was taken away from her mother and somehow had been left floating on a log. It was so upsetting, Aunt Rose and Aunt Nettie said, that they had never asked her about it again. It was a pity, though, because they could have learned a lot from her about the old days.

The Reese house was large, and three of the Reese girls—Nettie, Rose, and later on, Sophie, the youngest—came back home to live soon after they were married.

Sisters

They spent much of the time at their mother's. Nettie and Rose had no children; they separated from their husbands, who later died, and they stayed on with their mother. Ernestine remembers that they always dressed very well, like fashion plates, and everyone always noticed what they wore to church. The three women, Grandma Reese, Rose, and Nettie were very jolly and high-spirited; the children always like to go over to visit them.

Sophie stayed with her mother until her own children were of high school age, then rented a house. Among the Reese sons and daughters, only Sarah, Ernestine's mother, and one of her brothers who moved to Michigan ever owned a house. It was not until the next generation that the ties with the old homestead were broken, and many of the cousins bought their own homes.

The Baptist church is the center of social activity in Elm Park, and Grandma Reese was one of its first members. The girls sang in the choir, and the five oldest Reese sisters formed a singing group, "The Reese Sisters"; they sang in church on special occasions, and at other events. They wore formals and sometimes fancy costumes. They were very expressive young women, except for Sarah, who was shy. She always looked quite sober. An old picture shows Rose as serious-looking, Oralee as slim and beautiful, Ruth as pert, Nettie with a slight pout and a curl in the middle of her forehead (looking like a question mark, Rose remarked) and Sarah as rather prim.

Nettie had a beautiful contralto voice. It happened that a contralto was needed for a traveling operatic group and the manager heard about Nettie. He signed her up, and she toured with the group for about seven years. Her father did not want to let her go; he said, "I have lots of children, but none to spare." But he finally relented, and Nettie got to see the country and spent several years in New York. She was married at the time, but she and her husband had a somewhat tenuous relationship. A photograph of her first husband reveals a light-skinned, handsome man with a moustache and a riding hat. She claims that once when she was singing solo she had a vision of her husband, sitting in the front row. She felt dizzy, but kept on singing, as she had been trained. The next day she received word that her husband had died and she had to return home. She married again, and her second husband died in a TB sanitarium. She dreamed about the female mortician who arranged his funeral for several weeks before he died. Nettie complains that the woman got her accounts mixed up and even got the wrong date on her husband's death. She is still trying to charge Nettie for his funeral, although Nettie paid her long ago.

Despite her bad luck with husbands, Nettie carries her years lightly; she looks up to her older sister, Rose, fondly, but with a touch of sauciness. Rose is charming and seems to attract people to her. She dresses well—she has always had her clothes custom made—and wears a lot of jewelry. Her husband was a gentleman; Ernestine has never heard her say anything bad about him. He gave her expensive rings and necklaces, which she keeps locked up upstairs. She will not let anyone else up there. He died many years ago, and ever since Ernestine can remember, Rose has lived at the Reese place, first with her mother, then with her sister.

Oralee Collins and Ruth Davis, the two oldest girls, both had many children and died fairly young. Oralee was the beauty of the family before she had so many children and got so big; Ruth had been the comedienne and was well-liked. Her children also grew up to be very outgoing and sociable. But Ruth and Oralee died, after replenishing the population beyond the call of duty, leaving their less prolific sisters to carry on as a trio. The three sisters still get together every two weeks to practice; they recently sang at the Woman's Day program at the Elm Park Baptist Church and were billed as "The Famous Reese Sisters."

The youngest two Reese sisters never became a part of the singing group. Katherine had a beautiful voice and used to sing solos in church, but she was nine years younger than the next sister, and by the time she was old enough to join them they were already an established group. Even later on, after Oralee and Ruth died, she did not sing with the others.

A Tradition of Funerals   Katherine married a prominent man, who was a Mason, and she was active in the Eastern Star. She attended church faithfully, and when she died, the entire community united to give her a fine funeral. All the church groups—the Mother's Board, the Deacons and Deaconesses, the Gospel Choir, and the Senior Choir—went together and brought loads of food. They all sympathized deeply: there was a warm feeling toward the Reese family, especially toward the older members, who were socially active. It had been the same when Grandma Reese died: the house was full of people and they had every kind of food imaginable. In those days they held wakes in the home, and her body was there for viewing. Now, of course, wakes are held in one of the two prosperous-looking funeral homes in Elm Park. The funeral parlor that Ernestine's family patronizes is run by a couple who were born in Elm Park and who know all the families in the neighborhood. They know just what to do for a family at the time of a death.

I met the funeral director at the wake held for Howard Davis, who died not long after the fifth annual reunion. The director was a self-confident man, aware of his power. In his well-appointed office a sign read: "It's nice to be important, but more important to be nice."

At the wake, Rose sat with me in an alcove at the front of the room and pointed out various people as they viewed the body. She said that Howard had been a nice man and she was reminded of her own husband's death and how "shook-up" she had been. She felt hurt because she had not been with her nephew when he died. His wife had not even informed his sisters when he died. She called Uncle Alfred's wife, who lived downstairs at Aunt Rose's, and the news went out from there. Although he was a cousin and no longer lived there, Howard was still a Reese and merited a Reese funeral in Elm Park.

GOLDEN WEDDING

Behind the Scenes   The same couple who handles the Reese funerals made arrangements for Ernestine's parents' golden wedding anniversary celebration. They decided there should be a "wedding," with sisters and brothers, daughters, sons, sons-in-law, and grandchildren in attendance. The invitations were printed in gold, the bride was going to wear gold, and the female attendants were wearing green. Still, there was a great deal of consultation necessary about whether the dresses were to be bought or made and about the right shade of green. After the ceremony, there was to be a reception, for which Sarah herself was preparing the refreshments.

After the invitations were printed and all arrangements were made for the last Sunday in September, Ernestine's father disappeared. He had apparently driven off to visit some of his relatives in Michigan; he does that occasionally to get out of the city. He suffers from asthma and likes to go where the air is cleaner. They all laughed about how he had taken off: Sally had seen him, with paper bags and odds and ends, "just like a child from the country." Sarah was upset; she already had to have the date of the celebration changed once because she forgot to check with the minister and there was something else going on at the church. She just could not change it again. Sally, her second oldest daughter, felt that her mother should give up the idea of a big celebration and have a small dinner at home. She pointed out that her father would have to sit down in the reception line because of ill health, and "You won't ever get Mother to sit down; she'll be trying to see that all the people are served." Sarah was making too many elaborate preparations for the reception, and most of the food would be wasted. "Their people" would not eat a lot of those things she prepared; they prefer "soul food." But Sarah had spent all her life creating beauty for other people; now she was most happy doing the same thing for her own family.

Ernestine's father got back in time to hold the ceremony as planned. Cousin Benjamin, his sister's son, was to have been best man for the "wedding," but he could not make it on time and so Charles Reese, Sarah's brother's son "stood up" for his uncle. The women attendants looked beautiful and serene in green; Sarah was stunning in gold. Everyone was under a terrific strain because of the many preparations and last minute rush; there were, fortunately, some moments of relief, such as when Ernest Johnson gave his wife an extended passionate kiss. Everyone was surprised, and a humorous murmur ran through the audience. Ernestine said she did not know her father "had it in him."

Afterward, everyone in the Johnson family was tired for several days. Ernestine and her sisters had helped with the food for the reception, besides getting themselves and their children ready. Relatives had come from all over—fourteen cousins even came from Ohio—and they all had to be fed. Cousin Benjamin came in time to see the ceremony, as well as Ernest Johnson's first wife's nieces and nephews— Margaret's and Lawrence's stepbrothers and sisters—who gave 50 dollars to the couple. Lawrence could not come, but Margaret was one of the attendants. Most of the Davises were there, but of the Collinses, only Ruby was present. The relatives all pitched in and got the household articles and gifts back to the house in no time. The Johnsons received many, many gifts and 700 dollars from various relatives and church groups.

After the reception there was an informal gathering at the Johnson's home. Ernest Johnson was bouncing around, having a good time, although they had to take him out somewhere to get liquid for intravenous feeding. Ernestine and her sisters looked at old pictures of their parents when they were young and of Ernestine, Margaret, and their mother when all of them were young.

Elm Park: Old Times and New   Ernest Johnson's family came from around

Nashville, Tennessee, but Ernest grew up in Elm Park. All his family used to live there, but they have moved away. Ernest courted his second wife, Sarah, back when the streets were muddy ruts, with horse and buggy. He still jokes about going to see the little "country girl." Because the Reeses and the Johnsons both lived in Elm Park, the families were better acquainted than was the case with most of the in-laws of the Reeses. Two Reese cousins later married Johnsons also.

Ernest and Sarah Johnson went to work for a wealthy family as a domestic couple soon after they were married. Ernest was chauffeur and gardener, Sarah was cook and housekeeper. Margaret and Ernestine were left with a baby-sitter, an elderly woman who was a deaconess in the church, while their parents spent weekdays and nights at their employers' home. Later, when the two younger girls came along, Mrs. Johnson changed to day work and did catering on the side, and Mr. Johnson went to work at a local bakery. They saved enough money to buy a house in Elm Park; they had an extra oven and other appliances installed in the back for Sarah's work. Their life together was far from easy, but they have remained together through their 50th anniversary.

Ernestine's father had the upstairs made into an apartment and has tried to get one of his daughters to stay there. But none of the girls wants to live at home. Margaret left long ago, because she could not agree with her father's old-fashioned ideas about how girls should be brought up. Sally lives with her in-laws, a close-knit group, and Ernestine prefers to live in the city. She would not want to live out there "in the middle of nowhere, with no transportation." Susan and her husband bought a house of their own.

It was a big event when Susan bought a house in Elm Park. All of the other cousins either rent or have bought homes elsewhere; apparently Susan is carrying on the family tradition in Elm Park. That first Thanksgiving, all the Johnsons had dinner at Susan's home, setting a precedent. Previously, Sarah had always cooked the Thanksgiving dinner. I was invited to dinner, along with two couples who were friends of the family. The house, an older one, was tastefully decorated and furnished; the table was handsomely set. Both Ernestine and Susan have learned much from their mother about decor and serving; Ernestine has showed me pictures of centerpieces she has designed for holidays, and on every festive occasion her house is appropriately garnished for the season.

The dining room was rather crowded, with all the grandchildren and five outsiders; Sally came after dinner, announcing that she was on a diet. At the table, Ernestine's father looked around and said, "To think, we caused all this." After dinner, Sally showed movies of the 50th anniversary and of the reunion of her in-laws in Philadelphia, which she had attended that year.

Ernestine's father was attempting to be his usual jovial self, but was obviously rather weak and unwell. When he heard I was at the University, he quipped, "I go there, too; I study asthma." He talked about accompanying a friend who was recuperating from an illness to Arizona, but his family discouraged that. He could not take care of himself, much less someone else. He complained about being alone, with none of his children around and no one to talk to. He said his wife worked too hard. She had roasted two turkeys that day, besides the capon she had brought to the dinner. Still, he was proud of her, bragging that she was the best cook in the country.

Ernest Johnson laments the changing times. His family has all left and the Park is changing rapidly. Old houses are being torn down and new ones are springing up; new people are flocking in, and no one seems to know anyone. The churches are still large and prospering, as are the two funeral parlors, but there are no good stores or restaurants, and the one small grocery store has high prices. But worst of all, the old families have split up; the children are all grown and have business elsewhere. Only on special occasions when everyone gets together do you feel you are a part of a family.

A FINE AFFAIR

Setting the Stage   Early on the day of the Reese reunion Ernestine and I were on the way to Cousin Arlen's house. Ernestine had promised to be there by eight and I had offered to take her there and then on to the park. Neither of us had much sleep the night before: she had been calling people and working on signs and I was at a garage, trying to get my car back in time for the next day. It had been promised for six o'clock Saturday evening; I finally got it at three o'clock Sunday morning. The body shop, was Black-owned and operated, and when the owner found out how important it was that I have the car by Sunday, he stayed on through the night with his men to finish it. Their wives and girlfriends joined them; I bought some beer and we were a convivial group amidst the banging and scraping and the smell of grease and paint. But I was somewhat groggy at seven in the morning, and I had difficulty finding Arlen's house, which was in the area cut up by the Expressway.

Cousin Arlen's wife and two sons went along to the park to help set things up. His wife did not get out of the car, but one of the boys helped Ernestine move tables for awhile. Then his mother called him and she and the boys went back home to get their picnic lunch ready. Ernestine asked Benjamin, her ten-year-old, to help her; then she sent him on an errand and continued lugging tables around alone. Arlen was setting up his charcoal burner; he called to Ernestine to wait until he could help her. She said, "All right," but went on doggedly moving tables. She arranged tables around a large concrete platform, where there was to be dancing. Last year the tables had been scattered, and there had been no central focus.

Ernestine spread out white paper on the picnic tables, put some crepe paper streamers on the corners, and placed large artificial flowers in the centers. She set up signs on the tables, reading "The Johnson Family," "Charles (Reese) and Family," "Arlen (Collins) and Family," and so on. And so the stage was set.

While Ernestine was working on the tables, the disc jockey arrived with his wife and his equipment. He set up the amplifier and speakers, then started the music and kept it up throughout most of the day, at high volume. Last year, one of Aunt Sophie's sons had brought his portable record player; a group of the younger set had clustered around his table and sang. A few of the menfolk had started a ballgame; others were playing cards and some of the younger folk went swimming. Everyone was doing his own "thing," and there was very little feeling of being together as a group. This year, the music and the platform would be the focal points. Everyone would prefer to dance on the concrete, and they could not escape the music. In addition, there was to be a program, with the "DJ" as master of ceremonies. The program was well planned, with something for all age groups, and the natural showmanship of the Reese family was to be given full play.

The Participants   The first of the guests to arrive was Cousin Anne and her husband and family; her two sisters, Laura and Verona arrived soon after, also with their husbands. Verona brought her teen-age children, who participated actively in the events for the young people during the day. The remaining living Davis sister arrived much later, just as Ernestine and I were leaving; the deceased Davis girl was represented by several of her children. None of the Davis brothers came; two of them were apparently discouraged from coming by their wives.

Anne and Verona helped Ernestine with the preparations; Cousin Ruby arrived and also pitched in. They are all heavy, but buoyant women, and the tone of the day was set by their arrival. Ernestine was the behind-the-scenes manager: she set the stage, now the action began.

Laura was not so jolly as her sisters. Soon after her arrival she hurried over to Ernestine and announced, "Somebody called Arlen's wife and complained that the Collinses and the Davises are taking over." Ernestine replied, "Taking over what? This is a family affair." Laura went on, "Well, you know how people are: they don't want to give up any money unless they like what they're getting for it." At first Laura was critical of the arrangements, but as the day wore on she became mollified.

Ernestine's mother arrived after church; her father did not come, saying that he did not like driving on the Expressways. I sat with Sarah during most of the day, and she pointed out various relatives as they arrived. She kept looking for Sophie, her "baby sister"; soon Sophie, a very large, ebullient "baby sister" arrived in good spirits. Although she did not join the dancers later on, I saw her dance a few steps at her table now and then. Her sons and daughters and their wives and husbands were there, arriving early, but her husband was not. Her son's in-laws were there, however: the father looking distinguished, with a greyed goatee and a sombrero. Two of Ernestine's uncles, Otis and Samuel, arrived together with their respective wives, wearing bright-colored sport shirts. They had just returned from a trip to Hawaii that morning, Sarah informed me. Rose and Nettie came later with Uncle Alfred and his wife, completing the roll of the living Reese brothers and sisters.

In the older generation, the Reese men brought their wives, but husbands of Reese women did not come, asserting their independence of their wives' family. Among the cousins, on the other hand, wives brought their husbands, but in several instances Reese men were kept from coming to the reunion by their wives, or else they came without their wives. By this generation, the family line is established, the women tending to dominate in matters of family, and with tension developing between sisters and wives. An exception is Ernestine's sister, Sally, who attended her husband's family reunion in Philadelphia on the same day instead of the Reese gathering. Her husband and his father and brothers own a business jointly and Sally lives with her in-laws. At the Reese reunion, Reese women tended to be more active and husbands were content to remain in the background and "let them have their day." Arlen Collins was the only male cousin who took an active role in the proceedings; however, his wife kept him busy at their family table much of the time.

There were some generational differences that had to be handled at the outset if things were to go smoothly. Sarah complained about the loud music and criticized the dress of some of the younger set: bell-bottom pants, mini skirts, "mod" glasses, vests, "slouch" hats and cowboy hats. Ernestine immediately went up to talk to the "DJ" and soon some swinging religious music was playing with Sarah humming along. After that she seemed more accepting of the rock and jazz.

A Lively Group, Young and Old   The older generations were active "swingers," each in their own way. Among Ernestine's generation, elaborate hairpieces, stylish clothing, and highly extroverted social relations were the rule. Their offspring tended to be more reserved in their behavior but not in their dress, with "Afro" hairstyles, dashikis, and "mod" clothing dominating. There were good dancers in all generations, but the youth usually danced special "steps," while occasionally their parents would just "cut loose." The youngest children seemed to be the center of attention. They danced the "Popcorn," a rather stiff, jerky step that was popular at the time, with skill. They performed well in the contests that were held in the afternoon; Ernestine's son Benjamin won first prize and came over to our table beaming with pride.

All age groups participated in the dance contest and there was a set of prizes for each. One or two of the older women "let go" and were greeted by amusement mixed with admiration. Even the smallest children, some of them barely able to walk, danced, receiving much encouragement. The Collins were prominent in this part of the program: one of Ruby's sons directed a group of young people who danced in an ensemble. They evidently had practiced and kept together quite well, weaving back and forth in a line.

Ruby read a statement about the picnic and a request for "volunteers" for next year; then she proceeded to read off the names of the "volunteers." Ernestine had written out the statement and Ruby had difficulty reading it, stumbling over some of the words. Everyone agreed that Ernestine should have read it, but her voice did not carry well. She had first showed the statement to Arlen, to Anne, and to Laura to get their opinions; now she wished she had given it to Ruby the night before. After the announcement, Arlen gave away the pen and pencil sets to the graduates. He gave a short speech, saying how proud they all were and that he hoped his two sons, who were among the graduates, would do better than he had.

Out of the five Collins boys, three were present that day: Arlen and his wife and family, Bobby and his wife, and Arnold, whose wife did not come. Cousin Raymond and Vanessa stayed home again this year, as did Joseph, who lived in Michigan. Four out of the five living Collins sisters were there with their husbands and families. Ruby and her brother, Arlen Collins, of course, played central roles in the proceedings.

The Davises also participated whole-heartedly in the reunion, but despite their wide range of experience in social affairs, they did not play a part in its organization. None of the Davis boys was there; apparently their wives kept them at home.

Among the other cousins, Ernestine was the only one who took an active role in the planning and execution of the day's events.

Everyone was happy about how the reunion turned out and said it was a fine affair, much nicer than last year. They said they felt much closer together this year and praised Ernestine and the others. Ernestine had remained in the background throughout the day, but buzzed around to all the tables, talking to everyone and making arrangements. She had not eaten anything, claiming she was not hungry. Her children and I ate with her mother.

By four o'clock, Ernestine and I were both very tired. She could not find Benjamin, but she decided to leave, anyway, and let him stay with his grandmother that night. On the way back, I remarked to her that there was a wide variety of personalities among her relatives, and they were all interesting people. She laughed and said nothing; Ernestine had heard enough of Reeses and reunions until the next year.

REFLECTIONS ON "REUNION"

The insufficiency of the term "family" is evident in the organization of Ernestine's kin. She belongs to several overlapping kin groups, each of which has its own membership, characteristic celebrations, and unification rituals. First, Ernestine and her children celebrate the children's birthdays separately; then Ernestine, her parents, and her sisters and their families come together at Thanksgiving, formerly at the parents, recently at the home of the youngest daughter who has assumed ownership of a house in Elm Park (in an apparent continuation of the tradition of the first Thanksgiving). On Mother's Day, Ernestine's half-sister and brothers are included in the celebration, since all look to Sarah as their mother. At weddings of Johnson girls, the Johnson side is in evidence as the "original" affinals; at funerals, all relatives—the entire "kindred," as well as friends—attend, either in person or by communication. The Reese Reunion, based on the group of Reese sisters and brothers and their descendants, is the culmination for Ernestine of the yearly festivals. She is seen encouraging family unity and guaranteeing the continuance of the line by encouraging the participation of the young. In all of these groups, Ernestine is clearly aware of the boundaries and criteria for membership, although they of course overlap; they serve various purposes for members and provide different types of identification, preparing the children for a firm, multi-faceted social identity.

The women form the central core of Ernestine's various kin groups, and through them, children are given important positions and play crucial roles. The tension between the generations is muted as everyone realizes that the young are the inheritors of a proud and vital family tradition. The celebrations become more elaborate, as ties threaten to become more tenuous, for each kin group in the child's life plays an important role as annually the careers of individuals are recorded, important ties are renewed, and identity is reaffirmed. Nothing is left to the vagaries and good will of individuals alone; for as the Black person well knows, only through commitment to "one's own" can one find oneself.

7 / The Black extended family

In *Lifelines* I have described a limited number of families in Chicago. As a small-scale, intensive study it can be compared with other accounts to produce generalizations about the Black family. In the process of abstraction, much of the detail that comprises the lives of Black people is unfortunately lost; however, a compensation for such loss is the emergence of salient features of Black life in America.

To be sure, Black communities and families vary in the degree to which they share values with other groups. The question of cultural boundaries asserts itself: how do we define Black culture? In looking at culture as a *set of life-ways* (composed of elements such as language, technology, social roles, belief systems) rather than as a group of people possessing a culture, we can for any society construct a *serie*s of cultural boundaries that are permeable (allow members to cross over) and that crosscut each other. Some of these boundaries encompass nearly a total society, others transcend it. In U.S. society, cultural components such as the English language, political ideologies, and religious beliefs transcend national limits as well as those of ethnic and other social groups,[1] integrating large numbers of communities and at the same time differentiating them from others. Then there are elements such as dialects, social statuses, and particular roles and values that unify and differentiate on a smaller scale. St. Clair Drake,[2] Frazier,[3] and others describe some of the differentiating factors among Blacks. Harriet's comments concerning "our people" (in Chapter 4) coincide with ways in which "old" Black families in Chicago separated themselves socially from Southern immigrants in the 1920s and 1930s,[4] their hostility being largely a result of fear of competition for jobs. By the time of Drake's study (1945), some of the latter had become "respectable upper class," as he designates those in high social positions, indicating that if

[1] I am following here Fredrik Barth's definition of ethnic groups as social groups whose membership share a common origin and a field of communication and interaction, and which distinguishes itself and is distinguished by others from other like groups; it should be noted that this definition is based on social rather than on cultural criteria. (Ethnic Groups and Boundaries, Little, Brown, 1969, p. 11.)

[2] St. Clair Drake and Horace R. Cayton, *Black Metropolis: A Study of Negro Life in a Northern City*, Vol. II. New York: Harper & Row, 1945.

[3] E. Franklin Frazier, *Black Bourgeoisie*, New York: Macmillan, 1957.

[4] Allan H. Spear, *Black Chicago: The Making of a Ghetto*. Chicago: University of Chicago Press, 1931.

in fact there were differences, in this instance they were probably more economic than cultural.

While all Black communities or social groups do not fall within a particular set of cultural boundaries, perhaps certain unifying characteristics can be identified that reflect a common history and set of experiences shared by Black Americans. Thus, while the Black population is heterogeneous, Black culture is that medium through which a group of people in our society communicate and with which they identify as a group, while identifying with other groups on other bases.

In his still provocative work, *The Myth of the Negro Past*, Herskovits[5] cites studies that he believes show the survival of African culture and social organization in Black communities in the United States. For example, the casual attitude toward legal marriage and divorce reported by Frazier[6] and Powdermaker[7] are said to derive from African social forms in which separation and remating are "taken for granted" and in which marriage is *merely* an agreement between families.[8] (It should be noted here that such an agreement involves much bargaining, social recognition, and exchanges between kin groups, which are frequently the corporate groups that are politically dominant in the community.) Aside from the question of origin, it is clear that among the Chicago families, at least, although legal marriage is important, it is often subordinated to other considerations, some of these being the development of a mutually satisfactory arrangement between a man and a woman, the maintenance of strong mother-son and mother-daughter ties, and the preservation of a woman's domestic authority. Further, divorce may be viewed as a concession to respectability, as Powdermaker and Frazier report. Thus, Lucille and Sylvester decided to divorce their respective spouses only when they were planning to marry; and in at least one instance there was evidence that a second marriage had not been preceded by divorce (aside from Lucille's Uncle John, who "married" many times without the benefit of divorce), because the missing spouse had long been out of sight and mind. This reflects a refreshingly practical attitude toward the conventions, which, however, is not shared by all Blacks. Among the "upper middle class" families Powdermaker describes,[9] as well as among Frazier's "Black Bourgeoisie"[10] and Drake's "respectable upper class,"[11] a strongly legalistic morality appears to dominate, while among the bulk of the Black population a more pragmatic view toward the legal institutions of the dominant society seems to prevail. Herskovits did not, perhaps, give due recognition to the effects of the Black experience in America on Black social organization; Rawick[12] argues against a "simple retention" of African social forms, while recognizing their role in the development of institutions during Slavery. Similarly, different economic and historical influences

[5] Melville J. Herskovits, *The Myth of the Negro Past*. Boston: Beacon Press, 1941.

[6] E. Franklin Frazier, *The Negro Family in the United States*. Chicago: University of Chicago Press, 1931.

[7] Hortense Powdermaker, *After Freedom: A Cultural Study in the Deep South*. New York: Viking, 1939.

[8] Herskovits, *The Myth of the Negro Past*, p. 173.

[9] Powdermaker, *After Freedom*.

[10] Frazier, *Black Bourgeoisie*.

[11] Drake and Cayton, *Black Metropolis*.

[12] George P. Rawick, *The American Slave: From Sundown to Sunup; The Making of a Black Community*, Conn.: Greenwood, 1972.

on Black Americans account for varying sociocultural expressions in subsequent history.

Are there values that all Black Americans espouse? Johnetta Cole[13] proposes "style" and "soul" as basic to Black culture. Both are well-represented in the families in this study, particular in those of Lucille (Chapter 1), Adrienne (Chapters 3 and 4), and Ernestine (Chapter 6). Other values may be recognized throughout this study as well as in Powdermaker's Mississippi families,[14] in Virginia Heyer Young's contemporary Southern families,[15] in Joyce Ladner's St. Louis study,[16] in the more extensive works of Frazier[17] and Billingsley,[18] and in early accounts of slaves, free men, and their descendants. Among these values are (1) a high value placed on children; (2) the approval of strong, protective mothers; (3) the emphasis on strict discipline and respect for elders; (4) the strength of family bonds; and (5) the ideal of an independent spirit. These values are reflected in social practices that are parallel to, but which differ significantly from, those in White communities. For example, adoption by relatives and neighbors is widely practiced in Black families. As Powdermaker[19] and Johnson[20] point out, Black foster parents do not try to keep their origins from foster children, nor is there a feeling that they are at a disadvantage because they are not their "real" children. This stems from the more comprehensive reach of the extended family, in which other adults besides parents take responsibility for children. Again, because relatives and friends often take in orphaned or rejected children as a matter of course, legal adoption is not as crucial in Black families as in most White families.

While children are valued, Black families are not usually as "child-centered" as White conjugal families. Rainwater[21] notes that among lower-income families, children are often left to "fend for themselves" and speaks of the lack of "deep psychological involvement" with children. Liebow[22] notices that fathers often do not interact affectionately with children when they are living in the home, although they do so when they see them less frequently. It should be remarked that "deep psychological involvement" is not an unmixed blessing, as demonstrated in the etiology of certain typically "middle-class" neuroses,[23] and it implies an indirect but per-

[13] Johnetta Cole, "Black Culture: Negro, Black and Nigger," *The Black Scholar*, Vol. 1, No. 8, June 1970, pp. 40–43.

[14] Powdermaker, *After Freedom*.

[15] Virginia Heyer Young, "Family and Childhood in a Southern Negro Community," *American Anthropologist*, Vol. 72, No. 2, April 1970, pp. 269–288.

[16] Joyce Ladner, *Tomorrow's Tomorrow: The Black Woman*. Garden City, New York: Doubleday, 1971.

[17] Frazier, *The Negro Family in the United States*.

[18] Andrew Billingsley, *Black Families in White America*. Englewood Cliffs, N.J.: Prentice-Hall, 1968.

[19] Powdermaker, *After Freedom*.

[20] Charles S. Johnson, *Shadow of the Plantation*. University of Chicago Press, 1934.

[21] Lee Rainwater, "Crucible of Identity: The Negro Lower-Class Family," in *The Negro-American*, eds., Talcott Parsons and Kenneth B. Clark. New York: Houghton Mifflin, 1965, pp. 160–204.

[22] Elliot Liebow, *Talley's Corner: A Study of Negro Streetcorner Men*. Boston: Little, Brown, 1967.

[23] Arnold Green, "The Middle-Class Male Child and Neuroses," in Norman W. Bell and Ezra F. Vogel, ed., *A Modern Introduction to the Family*. New York: The Free Press, 1960, pp. 563–572.

vasive control over individuals with whom one is in daily contact. While Black mothers and fathers seek to protect their young, they do not try to "co-opt" them or to keep them as children for long. They are regarded as potential adults, because they will be forced to handle complex experiences at an early age. They often learn by observing and listening to adults, who go about their own business, apparently ignoring them, rather than by means of special attention: except when they need to be disciplined. Adults show they care by taking care of children, providing them with social supports, and by teaching them to behave. In a large family, particularly, those rewards that children receive—whether affection, attention, or more tangible things—must be sought and earned. Of course, this varies from family to family, but even in those families where children are more in evidence, the adults unquestionably rule.

An historical view of Black values under the regime of Slavery can be found in Frederick Douglass' autobiography. Taken from his mother, Douglass was raised by his grandmother from whom he was also separated at an early age. Yet he kept the two women—each of whom in her own way had tried to shield him from the terrors of slavery—vivid in his consciousness, attributing his later pursuit of intellectual achievements to the fact that his mother, whom he rarely saw, could read! Although he had not seen her for years, he suffered deeply when his grandmother was turned out to fend for herself because she was no longer useful to her master. Douglass describes the relationship of younger to older slaves on the plantation, whom they addressed as "Uncle" as a sign of respect: "There is not to be found among any people a more rigid enforcement of the law of respect to elders than is maintained among them."[24]

In her study of the Black woman, Ladner[25] examines the evidence from accounts of lives of slaves and concludes:

> Even when separation was apparent and fathers and mothers found themselves unable to prevent it, there was evident a profound feeling that the family would one day be united . . . This strong bond also transcended actual separation, because families were not reunited, memories and grief about kinsmen remained strong.

Thus, while individual families were broken up, the *concept* of family was operative in the lives of Slaves; while oppression leaves severe scars, perhaps certain values and concepts can be destroyed only by the extinction of a people.

Where and how did this strong feeling for family originate? Again, Herskovits[26] points to African origins: the kinship systems of African societies include patrilateral, matrilateral, and bilateral extended families, as well as lineages, while the "truncated" conjugal family is a product of Northern European culture. Herskovits' claim is difficult to validate, given the lack of information about tribal origins and the paucity of early evidence about families in the New World. Still, the argument is convincing: the view that Black people completely lost their concept of family, then recreated it as an *adaptation* to economic conditions seems harder to accept

[24] Frederick Douglass, *Life and Times of Frederick Douglass.* New York: Collier, 1892, p. 42.
[25] Joyce Ladner, *Tomorrow's Tomorrow*, p. 15.
[26] Herskovits, *The Myth of the Negro Past.*

than that of the continuance and modification of traditions that were, at least in essentials, strong in their memories.

The idea of the *adaptation* of a social form to a particular situation is fraught with difficulties: one can only argue after the fact, that it exists in a given environment, therefore it is adapted to it. There is no conclusive way of showing that it is *better* adapted than another might be under the same circumstances. Further, the *specific* conditions and the aims to which a social form is adapted must be indicated. These concerns can be illustrated by an analysis of a widely discussed condition of Black existence, namely, the relatively large number of female-headed households. As TenHouton[27] has documented, the higher rate of such households among Blacks is largely an artifact of the predominance of Black families in the urban setting, where matrifocal households are generally more common than in rural areas. Still, the situation exists and can be explained by a number of factors, including: (1) the relatively high fertility of Black women; (2) the low (men to women) sex ratio during the child-bearing age (due to the high mortality rate among young Black men); (3) the lack of permanent, well-paying jobs for men where money is the primary security; and (4) attitudes toward marriage and motherhood. It should be noted that the latter cultural variable is operative but not paramount. Taking these factors into consideration, it is apparent that Black women in an urban setting choose to have children, tolerating a degree of uncertainty in finding a suitable mate, rather than to remain childless. Even with increasing knowledge of birth control and easier access to abortion and adoption, most Black women choose to bear and raise their children. From one viewpoint, this behavior may be seen as adaptive for a minority in terms of population growth; from another, it may be seen as a hindrance to economic advancement. In any case, it is behavior that is reinforced by the high value placed on having children. Whether this value has directly contributed to the economic and social advancement of Black Americans is difficult to determine; but in the larger sense of lending dignity and worth to the person, as well as of strengthening the family, such a value is adaptive.

Matrifocal families or households have been described as adaptive or as dysfunctional, depending on the perspective;[28] a more tenable position is that in themselves they are merely the result of the shortage of men and the economic conditions in Black communities while, given these conditions, as a part of the larger family organization these living arrangements are highly functional. For a Black man, complete commitment to one household carries with it the risk of loss of pride if he loses his job or is unable to handle emergencies; further, the high fertility rate together with the higher death rate among young men means that there are more children per able-bodied man to support than in the White population. A solution to this problem that may be considered adaptive is the relative independence of men from a particular household, while they may be attached to a number of households in a variety of roles, contributing financial and emotional support. While these part-families put a strain on the women as the major sources of support, they can

[27] Warren D. TenHouten, "The Black Family: Myth and Reality," *Psychiatry*, Vol. 33, No. 2, May 1970, pp. 145–155.
[28] *Cf.* Ulf Hannerz, *Soulside: Inquiries into Ghetto Culture and Community.* New York: Columbia University Press, 1969.

be seen as advantageous in the context of the extended family, giving the adult woman domestic authority and the freedom to raise her children and conduct her relationships with men as she sees fit, with the larger family group as a contributing support and orientation.

Another advantage of part-families that has become apparent in my study is the role they may play in geographic and social mobility, as "outposts" of the family. Maya Angelou,[29] writer and choreographer, describes her experiences first in her grandmother's household in a small Southern town, which she shared with her brother and maternal uncle, then with her mother in St. Louis, and later with her father in California. She became aware of a broad range of situations (some of which were painful) and opportunities that she probably would not have encountered had she spent all her childhood in a conjugal family in her birthplace. Children in White families, which are integrated into social institutions through PTA, Booster Clubs, Boy and Girl Scouts, and other organizations learn social alternatives through these media, while Black children more often learn through their families and peer groups. While the influence of peer groups has been duly emphasized, the importance of the family has not been sufficiently recognized.

The Black family should not be labeled *apriori adaptive*, any more than any other family type; if a social form such as the extended family survives under a variety of conditions, the adjective "adaptable" is more applicable than "adaptive": the latter refers to a *response* in a situation, an adaptation. An institution is "adaptable" rather than "adaptive," because it changes in a relatively slow manner and in response to a complexity of economic and social forces. The ways in which an institution adapts in a particular situation can be specified, *viz.*, matrifocal households. The Black family has demonstrated adaptability throughout Black history: in the rural South, during migration to the North, and in Northern cities. It should not be viewed as an *ad hoc* response to a particular set of conditions, but as a continuing institution within whose scope adaptive responses such as matrifocal households originate and are given foundation.

It is essential to grasp the concept of the Black extended family as an institution; otherwise, certain types of behavior may be misunderstood or misinterpreted. In his treatment of the Black family, Rainwater[30] speaks of the lack of control mothers have over their households, giving as example the fact that older children have the right to come home at any time and stay there without contributing to the maintenance of the household. It should be stated that his right is often extended to grandchildren and to nieces and nephews whose mothers are deceased, as well as to other relatives. In extended families in Pakistan, such rights are taken for granted, as in similar family systems; this is a structural aspect of extended families, not a sign of lack of authority. In such systems, there may be a great deal of complaining about granting such rights (as in the case of Lucille's response to the actions of her brother's wife and child—and who would accuse her of lack of authority?); still, they are respected nevertheless, since they involve the integrity of the family institution.

As became apparent during my investigation in Chicago, the term "family" is

[29] Maya Angelou, *I Know Why the Caged Bird Sings*. New York: Random House, 1970.
[30] Rainwater, "Crucible of Identity."

ambiguous: to some of my respondents it referred to members of a household, while to others it included parents and brothers and sisters who were married and living elsewhere. My usage here is in reference to the effective kin group, whether occupying one or several households. "Extended family," then, refers to a more or less localized kin group in which active support is forthcoming; if such localized groups exist in several cities with some interaction among them, they can be characterized as branches, or extended families within the kindred or bilateral kinship network. Carol Stack has identified such groups—"co-residential and/or domestic units of cooperation"—among Chicago families she studied, although she does not use the term "extended family."[31] Elsewhere Stack describes "personal kindreds"— ego-centered networks of relatives and friends that differ for each individual.[32] Applying this concept to my data: Lucille's two sons appear to have such personal networks because they have different fathers. However, she attempts to integrate her children's kindred into one bilateral kinship network by involving them in each other's "personal kindred." Lois McCoy and her siblings related to a bilateral kindred, largely through the efforts of their stepfather's nephew, while Harriet chose not to activate her children's patrilateral ties. The element of personal choice here is clear, but it does not result in "ego-centered networks"; rather, it indicates a kind of "ambilateral" system. All of the individuals mentioned here are basically oriented to their mothers' (and to a lesser extent, their fathers') kin groups; while most children are the focus of an extensive network of friends, relatives, and fictive kin, their basic identity and security lie within a relatively limited and clearly bounded set of kin. The extended family, then, is surrounded and nourished by a larger social network, which forms its "community."

In some instances, as in Lucille Foster's family, the extended family appears to transcend wide spatial separation, maintaining a high degree of contact and support over long distances. As we have seen, Lucille considers herself an "orphan" revealing both the difficulties in integrating a family across long distances and the importance attached to close family relationships. This may be transitional: as her children grow up and marry and her own parents die, her family will more closely resemble others in the study.

To characterize the family system as extended does not imply that households consisting of husband, wife, and children are not predominant in Black communities, just as classifying the prevailing family system in the White population as conjugal is not to deny that the kindred may be important in some areas and among some families.[33] Further, the household make-up and the relative independence of households in rural, urban, and suburban areas and in different economic classes varies considerably in both populations. I have described families in a pre-

---

[31] Carol B. Stack, "The Kindred of Viola Jackson: Residence and Family Organization of an Urban Black American Family," in *Afro-American Anthropology: Contemporary Perspectives*, Norman E. Whitten, Jr., and John F. Szwed. New York: The Free Press, 1970, pp. 301–311.

[32] ———, "Black Kindreds: Parenthood and Personal Kindreds Among Urban Blacks," *Journal of Comparative Family Studies*, Vol. III, 1972, pp. 303–311.

[33] It should be noted, however, that even conjugal-based households stand ready to take in other relatives for varying lengths of time and that such relatives are more frequently found in Black households.

dominantly urban setting, where female-headed households are more common; however, my work in Chicago, and more recently in Southern Illinois indicates that even where the conjugal family is intact, it often exists as a unit in a larger family organization. Therefore, when Black families are classified together with White families of the same household membership, important differences may be submerged, such as the integration of the former into a larger social group.

The apparent fragility of conjugal ties in Black families may partly stem from a structural characteristic, namely, the solidarity of the extended family. Marriage, as we have seen, is the outcome of a series of negotiations based on an initial strong emotional attachment. Such attachments are precarious and resemble the "emotional friendships," as contrasted with primarily "instrumental friendships" described by Eric Wolf.[34] He asserts that emotional friendships are of special importance in societies with solidary kinship groups, providing "emotional release and catharsis from the strains and pressures of role-playing." Where there are strong kinship ties, daily interaction with close kin gives rise to emotional constraints and deeply ambivalent feelings; emotional friendships serve as an outlet for frustrated affection, even hostile feelings. Such friendship bonds carry an extra load, since the needs are so intense, and when they are not reinforced by strong social or economic considerations, are tenuous. Further, the solidary groups regard such friendships as a threat and attempt to limit them. Rainwater[35] has shown that peer groups attempt to thwart "tight" relationships between men and women; the same holds for families, particularly if there is a probability of marriage. This is especially the case if a man or woman is contributing economically to a family of orientation.

The characteristics of the friendships described by Wolf seem familiar: "Once a high intensity of friendship was attained, scenes of jealousy and frustration could be expected and the cycle would end in a state of enmity."[36] Because of the separation of the sexes among Latin peoples, these friendships are with members of the same sex; Black women, however, often refer to lovers as "friends;" and since a friendship characteristically includes instrumental exchanges among Blacks, one involving a married man or woman may compete with a marital tie. If a marriage is not based on strong economic interdependence—that is, if a woman and/or her family are important financial contributors—the conjugal tie may be threatened. On the other hand, a marriage in which a husband contributes substantially to the household may survive many extramarital affairs on either side.

The "play-kin" relationship is less intense and plays a somewhat different role. Serving as a compensatory tie, as the love relationship, it allows family members to "play at" roles that are in earnest in the family. It is a pleasure to be able to put off a request or to confer a favor voluntarily when family demands are obligatory. Earline, Lucille's "adopted" sister, took care of her father when he was sick, but rather grudgingly; on the other hand, she was gladly generous with her godchildren,

---

[34] Eric R. Wolf, "Kinship, Friendship, and Patron-Client Relations in Complex Societies," in Michael Banton, ed., *The Social Anthropology of Complex Societies*. Edinburgh: Tavistock Publications, 1966, pp. 1–22.

[35] *Ibid.*

[36] *Ibid.*, p. 12.

Lucille's sister's children. Merely conferring kinship titles signifies a feeling of obligation, however, if somewhat attenuated, just as a love relationship entails a responsibility. When feelings of obligation are expanded to include neighbors and close friends through fictive kinship ties and peer groups of various kinds, a complex community life emerges.

According to Wolf, the pressures and demands of a rich communal life frequently lead to envy and suspicion, which play a part in "maintaining the rough equality of life chances."[37] Quarrels and suspicions about infidelity, money, and intentions in general reflect dependency on the sometimes capricious whims of relatives and friends. One must always be on one's guard so that no one will take advantage. The strong needs for escape, especially among men, and the avoidance of permanent attachments with unlimited commitments underscore the heavy demands made on people with limited means. In this context, the drive to maintain one's privacy and independence become comprehensible. Yet the Black person realizes, fundamentally, that to be oneself implies sharing oneself with others.

Implicit in the organization of extended families is a humanistic value—that of deep involvement in the lives of many people. Among poorer families, sharing is more often in the form of small loans and gifts of money, as well as services, while in those with more financial security, often only social support and services are exchanged; in either case, sacrifices of time, energy, or money as well as sympathy and concern are expected and received. Sometimes demands cause resentments and conflicts among family members; but the sense of obligation is strong.

In my observation, Black culture is generally humanistic in orientation, and expresses a profound knowledge of the human condition. In particular, the approach to life's vicissitudes reflects this understanding. The Black person's suspicions of others, whether right or wrong, are more often based on knowledge of human nature than on ignorance; thus, although she is sometimes wrong in detail, on the whole Lucille takes a realistic view of Sylvester's state of affairs; Rachel's suspicions of Bradley were probably less well-founded, but then she was just beginning to learn about life.

Even when they fight and contend, Blacks respect those who communicate freely and clearly, expressing and sharing themselves. If people do not share, they must be made to, and the manipulation of people is open, direct, and often verbal, rather than indirect as in most White families. For this reason, among others, Blacks often accuse Whites of hypocrisy. Some of the children in Chapter 4 can be seen learning verbal manipulative skills. Much of the verbal abuse among Blacks, as pointed out by Kochman[38] and Abrahams,[39] is merely game-playing, for purposes of excitement and drama, to relieve tension and to influence people. Dean's threats and abusive language toward Lois and her mother were largely of this nature, directed toward gaining control over his son. Such attacks are usually not as

[37] *Ibid.*, p. 11.

[38] Thomas Kochman, "Rapping in the Black Ghetto," in *Perspectives on Black America*, ed. Russell Edno and William Strawbridge. Englewood Cliffs, N.J.: Prentice-Hall, 1970, pp. 23–39.

[39] Roger P. Abrahams, "Playing the Dozens," *Journal of American Folklore*, July-September 1962, pp. 209–220.

devastating to Blacks—who have been socialized to parry them—as they would be to one reared in a White middle-class family setting. Oftentimes such exchanges are repeated with relish: "He said so-and-so; then I said so-and-so," indicating who had gotten the best of whom or whether it was a draw.

An outsider, hearing terms such a "bad," "evil," "mean," "fool," "nigger," "whore," "bitch," and "motherfucker" might believe that the Black concept of human nature is a degraded one; however, it is becoming widely recognized that these are an indirect, satirical comment on the society that has tried to denigrate them rather than on Black people themselves. Self-doubt and pathological self-criticism exist—in Harriet, for example—as a bitter aftertaste of a history of encounters with racism. But, as Ladner maintains,[40] basically Black men and woman, sustained by their social environment, maintain a healthy balance of self-regard and self-criticism. Some of their idioms reflect an inversion of White values by which Blacks assert the beauty of the essential Black man and woman and of Black culture. The real pejorative is "cold"—"uninvolved," "callous," perhaps by implication, "White."

Some values of Black Americans have been modified with changing conditions. There is some evidence that relationships between parents and children and between men and women are increasingly egalitarian among Northern families, particularly in those that have migrated from the South, and that an other-worldly orientation is being replaced by a more secular one, reflecting a more accurate picture of the role of Blacks in American society. Still, it is largely a matter of emphasis and ideology, and Black institutions such as the family persist.

In relation to some values and institutions of the society at large—materialism, legalism and puritanism—Black people, especially those who are poor—have often shown a high high degree of pragmatism; here I would agree with Valentine,[41] that characteristics that Lewis[42] identifies as belonging to the "culture of poverty" are actually strategic responses in adaptation to White-dominated economic, politcal, and religious institutions. Yet the life choice of Black men and women involve far more than strategies for survival. Black Americans are resolute in their adherence to the system of values which they have maintained and developed—a way of life that has demonstrated adaptability and persistence in the face of great odds, carrying its bearers through a broad range of life experiences in a familiar, though often inhospitable, society.

[40] Ladner, *Tomorrow's Tomorrow.*

[41] Charles A. Valentine, *Culture and Poverty, Critique and Counter-Proposals.* Chicago and London: University of Chicago Press, 1968.

[42] Oscar A. Lewis, "The Culture of Poverty," *Scientific American*, Vol. 215, No. 4, 1966, pp. 19–25.

Recommended reading

Angelou, Maya, *I Know Why the Caged Bird Sings*. New York: Random House, 1970.
A well-known choreographer and actress tells her own story in a moving and literate account, giving a lucid picture of the importance of kin relations in her history.

Billingsley, Andrew, *Black Families in White America*. Engelwood Cliffs, N.J.: Prentice-Hall, 1968.
Dr. Billingsley's scholarly study of Black families reveals some of the strengths as well as the problems of Black family life in different social statuses.

Frederick Douglass, *Life and Times of Frederick Douglass*. New York: Collier, 1892.
The life history of a distinguished Black man during Slavery.

Drake, St. Clair and Horace R. Cayton, *Black Metropolis: A Study of Negro Life in a Northern City*, Vols. I and II. New York: Harper & Row, 1945.
A comprehensive description of the Chicago Black ghetto, its physical characteristics, social organization and processes.

Hannerz, Ulf, *Soulside: Inquiries into Ghetto Culture and Community*. Columbia University Press, 1969.
A stimulating and comprehensive account of Black ghetto life, which occasionally suffers from lack of clarity and incisiveness.

Herskovits, Melville, *The Myth of the Negro Past*. Boston: Beacon Press, 1947.
Although Herskovits at times seems to underestimate the importance of the American experience in the development of Black culture, his evidence for African survivals is nevertheless. impressive.

Keiser, R. Lincoln, *The Vice Lords: Warriors of the Streets*. New York: Holt, Rinehart and Winston, 1969.
A study in this series of a Black street gang in Chicago that reveals the organization and strength of social ties among young Black men.

Kunkel, Peter and Sara Sue Kennard, *Spout Spring: A Black Community*. New York: Holt, Rinehart and Winston, 1971.
Some interesting parallels and comparisons with the present study occur in this study of a Black community in the Ozarks, also in this series. See especially Chapter 5, "Families and Households" and Chapter 8, "Culture."

Ladner, Joyce A., *Tomorrow's Tomorrow: The Black Woman*. Garden City, N.Y.: Doubleday, 1971.
A penetrating, often shattering, account of the lives of young Black girls in a St. Louis ghetto.

Moody, Anne, *Coming of Age in Mississippi*. New York: The Dial Press, 1968.
The autobiography of a Mississippi Black girl, revealing the joys, hazards, and fearful responsibilities of childhood and young adulthood in the South.

145

Powdermaker, Hortense, *After Freedom: A Cultural Study in the Deep South*. New York: Atheneum, 1968.
A description of a Southern Black community in the 1930s, which gives an insight into family, sex roles, and relationships.

Rawick, George P., *The American Slave: A Composite Autobiography*; Vol. 1, "From Sundown to Sunup": The Making of the Black Community. Westport, Conn.: Greenwood Publishing Co., 1972.
Attempting to reconstruct Black social institutions under Slavery from contemporary accounts, historian Rawick characterizes an entire plantation as "a generalized extended kinship system," in which socialization was carried out with effectiveness and in which institutions were developed through conscious innovation and the modification of a tradition.

Spear, Allan H., *Black Chicago. The Making of a Negro Ghetto 1890–1892*. Chicago: University of Chicago Press, 1967.
An historical account of the Great Migrations and the development of the social and political institutions in the Black ghettos of Chicago.

Stack, Carol B., *All Our Kin*. New York: Harper & Row, 1974.
A study of a Black community in Illinois, which reveals significant similarities to the material in this work with regard to attitudes toward child-rearing practices, economic reciprocity, and household and family organization.

Whitten, Norman E., Jr. and John F. Szwed, *Afro-American Anthropology: Contemporary Perspectives*. The Free Press, 1970.
A collection of essays, the most pertinent to the present study being that by Carol Stack ("The Kindred of Viola Jackson: Residence and Family Organization of an Urban Black American Family," and Robert Blauner's statement concerning Black culture ("Black Culture, Myth or Reality?")